FIRST PUBLISHED 1946

BOOK
PRODUCTION
WAR ECONOMY
STANDARD

THE TYPOGRAPHY AND BINDING
OF THIS BOOK CONFORM TO THE
AUTHORISED ECONOMY STANDARD

FOREWORD

TWO remarkable characters are brought together in this volume—Balaam the son of Beor, and Jonah the son of Amittai. They were somewhat alike in one deplorable particular, each was willing that a vast number of souls should be sacrificed for some advantage to himself. With Balaam it was money; with Jonah it was his reputation! Balaam was a downright emissary of Satan, masquerading as a prophet of Jehovah for the sake of gain; Jonah, on the contrary, was a true man at heart, but somewhat of an untrained colt, sorely needing to learn important lessons in the school of God. From both Balaam and Jonah we may learn much: from the one, the danger of trafficking in unfelt truth; and from the other, the importance of entering into the divine sympathies while engaged in work for God. If we do not feel towards men as God feels, how can we be efficient as witnesses for Him?

God grant that the words we utter with our lips may at all times come from our very hearts!

Contents

Part I.

JONAH AND HIS EXPERIENCES.

Part II.

BALAAM.

(i) *Jonah and His Book*

IT has been remarked by others that the Book of Jonah is as singular amongst the books of the Old Testament as the Epistle of James is amongst the writings of the New.

The Old Testament is occupied largely with God's gracious purposes concerning Israel ; yet there we find the story of a special mission of mercy to Gentiles ! The New Testament unfolds the purposes of God concerning Christ and the Church, yet amongst the Apostolical epistles we find one addressed to the twelve tribes ! From Jonah's book we may learn that in the dispensation in which Israel was the centre of God's ways He nevertheless had a heart of compassion for those outside the chosen race. From James' Epistle we may gather that, although a change of dispensation has set in, and God is now engaged in gathering out sinners from all the nations for heavenly bliss in association with the risen Christ, He has not forgotten His ancient people.

Apart from the inspiration of the Spirit of God, the very existence of the Book of Jonah is difficult to understand. That a highly conservative people, who were accustomed to look down with contempt upon the uncircumcised, should admit such a book as Jonah's into the Sacred Canon is proof that it was given by God. However distasteful its contents might be to their prejudiced minds, Israel regarded the book as divinely authoritative.

No one could have written the Book of Jonah but the prophet whose name it bears. Another might conceivably have told of his mission to Nineveh and its amazing results ; but who but himself could have told of his conversation aboard ship, or who could have given the very words of his prayer to Jehovah in the fish's belly, and of his peevish complaints afterwards, and the gracious remonstrances of God with him ? In some later period in his life, when he had learned his lesson, Jonah was guided by the Holy Spirit to write his most interesting story, which reflects the deepest discredit upon the prophet himself, while containing the most wholesome instruction for all who seek to witness for God in any age. Surely no more frank confession of grievous faults was ever published !

4

Everyone shines brightly in the book of Jonah but the writer ! The heathen mariners were reluctant to deliver him up to death (Israel's leaders had no such scruples concerning the Lord Jesus) ; and they turned with sacrifices to the one true God when the storm so abruptly ceased. The King of Nineveh, with his nobles and people, trembled at the word of God, and humbled themselves before Him, thus averting the threatened judgment. The fish was obedient to its Creator, for when Jehovah spake to it, " it vomited out Jonah upon the dry land," (Jonah ii. 10).

And God—what shall we say of Him ? What consideration for the mariners ! What care of His disobedient servant during the mysterious three days ! What prompt response to the repentance of the wicked Ninevites ! What thoughtfulness for children and cattle ! What condescending remonstrances with His most faulty servant after all His dealings with him ! These records bring home to our hearts the greatness and graciousness of the God with whom we have to do.

The question has been raised whether the book of Jonah is sober history, or merely a " story " written by someone for a moral purpose. No question could be more evil, for it challenges the truthfulness of no less a person than the blessed Son of God. On various occasions in the course of His ministry He alluded to Old Testament records as pointing a warning to men of His own day. When defending the divine institution of marriage, He spoke of the creation of Adam and Eve as the first pair (Matt. xix. 4-5) ; He spoke also of the murder of Abel (Matt. xxiii. 35) ; of the flood (Matt. xxiv. 38) ; and of the destruction of Sodom and Gomorrha (Luke xvii. 29). To all these He added a twofold reference to Jonah. First to his preaching, and the repentance of the men of Nineveh. This was intended as a solemn rebuke to the heartless men who heard the voice of our Lord and heeded it not. Then He referred to Jonah's three days imprisonment in the belly of the fish. This was meant as a warning to our Lord's hearers that as Jonah disappeared from view for three days and three nights, so would the despised Greater than Jonah become lost to Israel and the world (Matt. xii. 39-41). For the prophet's strange experiences were typical of the death and resurrection of the Lord Jesus.

It is unthinkable that the all-knowing Son of God should seek to warn men by reference to the flood, the overthrow of Sodom and Gomorrha, and the experiences of Jonah if none of these things really happened. If the One to whom both writer and readers look for salvation from ruin is not to be trusted when speaking of mere historical events, how can we trust Him when He speaks of those things which belong to our eternal peace ? A man once urged upon me that he should be accepted as a " good Christian " even though he rejected the story of Jonah ! I refused the suggestion with indignation. He who casts doubt upon the trustworthiness of the Son of God courts disaster for himself, and is a peril to all who come under his influence. The hiss of the serpent is all around us. The dispensation has grown old, and the predicted apostasy draws near. Let us cleave confidently to Him who when on earth spake as no other ever spake (John vii. 6), and who concluded His public ministry with the emphatic and unmistakeable words of John xii. 49-50 : " I have not spoken from Myself ; but the Father which sent Me He gave Me commandment what I should say, and what I should speak. And I know that His commandment is life everlasting : whatsoever I speak therefore, as the Father hath said unto Me, so I speak."

(ii) *Jonah and His Experiences*

" THE prophet Jonah."   This is our Lord's own description of him in Matt. xii. 39 ; but the cursory reader of the book may be disposed to ask, " Where are the prophecies ? " Certainly Jonah's book differs in character from those of Isaiah and other prophets. Their rich and full unfoldings of glories yet to come are lacking in Jonah's chapters ; but prophecy is there nevertheless : the fact is that the man himself, and Jehovah's remarkable dealings with him constitute a prophecy, and that of a deeply interesting character. In this unfaithful witness God gives us an illustration of His ways with the unfaithful nation to which he belonged. Thus there is a prophetic as well as moral instruction in the book of Jonah. It is a prophecy in picture.

" The word of Jehovah came unto Jonah the son of Amittai, saying, Arise, go to Nineveh, that great city, and cry against it ; for their wickedness is come up before Me." Jonah had already been entrusted with messages from Jehovah to Israel (2 Kings xiv. 25) ; now he has the unique distinction of being sent " far hence unto the Gentiles " (Acts xxii. 21). It is an unspeakable honour to be a messenger for God at any time. Have we all learned this ? Are we all in the spirit of Isaiah's words, " Here am I, send me " ?

Jonah, alas, was not well pleased to be sent to preach to Gentiles. He had been God's willing mouthpiece to proclaim good things to his own nation ; but a foreign nation—a Power withal dangerously hostile to Israel—that was a different matter ! Even after the Holy Spirit came from heaven consequent upon the exaltation of the Lord Jesus, Peter had scruples about carrying the Gospel to the Roman garrison in Caesarea ! (Acts x.). These lines are written while many Powers are engaged in the most terrible war the world has yet known. National feelings are running high ; and even Christians, although divinely separated by grace from the world and united to Christ in heaven, are sometimes influenced by what is being said and done around them. How slow are we to learn the blessed meaning of God's " whosoever " ! The heart of God most assuredly goes out equally to men of every country and colour, and He desires that they may " be saved, and come to the knowledge of the truth " (1 Tim. ii. 4). Do we desire also ?

Jonah, on hearing the word of Jehovah, made a dash for the port of Joppa. He would flee from His presence ! Vain effort ! Psa. cxxxix. stresses this very definitely. But why did Jonah refuse the divine commission to preach to the men of Nineveh ? Chap. iv. 2 tells us. The known goodness of God was his difficulty. He was sure that if the Ninevites repented of their wickedness God would show mercy. In that case Jonah felt that his dignity would be affected—to proclaim a judgment which was not executed ! Rather let a whole vast city perish than that his credit should suffer ! It seems almost incredible that a man born of the Spirit could be so self-important and behave so contemptibly ! This story, so simply told, is written as a warning to us all. If we get out of communion with God, His tender compassions become foreign to us ; harsh feelings develop ; and we behave abominably. We shall doubtless meet Jonah in the glory of God ere long (like ourselves, a sinner saved by grace) ; but meantime let us seek to be as unlike him as possible in our service and testimony for God.

It seemed quite providential that a ship was about to sail for Tarshish when the wayward prophet reached Joppa, but circumstances are not always a safe guide for God's saints. Let us never forget this. It does not follow that because circumstances fit in nicely with our wishes that God has ordered things so for us. Jonah, tired with his journey like Elijah after his flight from Jezebel, went below, and was soon in a sound sleep. " But Jehovah sent out a great wind into the sea, and there was a mighty tempest in the sea, so that the ship was like to be broken." At a later date, Paul was exposed to a great storm in the same Mediterranean Sea, but the contrast between Paul and Jonah when danger arose is very striking (Acts xxvii). The Apostle was travelling towards Rome in accordance with the Lord's words in Acts xxiii. 11 : " Be of good cheer, for as thou hast testified of me in Jerusalem, so must thou also bear witness of Me at Rome " ! With these words ringing in his ears, Paul moved confidently. His moral dignity throughout the storm was wonderful. He almost took command of the ship, even though both owner and " skipper " were on board. " Sirs, ye should have hearkened unto me." Yet Paul was no ordinary passenger, he was a prisoner in custody ! By contrast, Jonah was a mean figure amongst the ship's company, and fully merited the rebuke of the master (chap. i. 6).

Let us not miss the lesson of this contrast. A Christian walking in communion with God is on a high level, but a Christian out of communion is a degraded spectacle. Men respect the one, but they despise the other. The one will be a blessing to men ; but the other may be a stumbling-block, and even a curse !

(iii) *Jonah and Christical*

THE Lord's words in Matt. xii. 39-40 shew plainly that He regarded Jonah's descent into the depths as a foreshadowing of His own impending death. " As Jonah was three days and three nights in the whale's belly, so shall the Son of man be three days and three nights in the heart of the earth." But how great the contrast between Jonah's experience, and that of our Lord ! Our Lord tasted death in all its terrible reality as the righteous judgment of God against sin—your sin and mine, beloved reader. Not so Jonah. The perverse critics of the Lord asked again for a sign in Matt. xvi., and again He referred them to the story of Jonah. But He rebuked their hypocrisy thus : " When it is evening, ye say, it will be fair weather : for the sky is red. And in the morning, foul weather to-day, for the sky is red and lowering. Ye can discern the face of the sky : but can ye not discern the signs of the times ? " It was indeed " fair weather " for the Jewish people at that moment, for the Sun was shining brightly, in their midst ; but ' foul weather ' was approaching—judgment from God for their evil unbelief. " He left them and departed "—significant words ! The doom of the people was certain.

Jonah is an interesting type of Christ. He belonged to Galilee. Gath-Hepher was not far distant from Nazareth. The Jewish

Counsellors were in error when they said to Nicodemus : " Search and look : for out of Galilee ariseth no prophet " (John vii. 52) ; but probably they ignored Jonah because his mission was to Gentiles a thought abhorrent to their pride.

When Jonah bade the seamen cast him into the sea, he was apparently not afraid to die. Backslider though he was, he had not lost all confidence in God. Jehovah could do (and did) great things for His erring servant. Here we must contrast Jonah with our blessed Lord. Disobedience led the one into the depths ; Obedience led the Other.

" Jonah was in the belly of the fish, three days and three nights." God says so ; let no-one doubt His word. In 1 Cor. xv. 4 we read that Christ was raised the third day according to the Scriptures ! No Old Testament prophecy says this definitely. Hos. x. 2 may occur to our minds ; but if Christ is intended there, the language is certainly vague. But He who knew all things from the beginning kept Jonah three days and three nights in the depths in order to present to us an expressive picture of the death and resurrection of the Lord Jesus. The " third day " is found also in the story of Isaac the son who was raised from the dead " in a figure." (Heb. xi. 19), saw the place of his typical death and resurrection on the third day of his journey with his father (Gen. xxii. 4).

Thus Jonah was " cast into the deep, in the midst of the seas," and was constrained to say, "all Thy billows and Thy waves passed over me." His unfaithfulness brought him to this ; nevertheless the fruit for others of all that he passed through was marvellous. The heathen mariners, who at first prayed every man to his god, were brought to know Jehovah ; for Jonah, although in the path of disobedience, did not hesitate to say, " I am a Hebrew, and I fear Jehovah, the God of heaven, who made the sea and the dry land." The mariners forthwith cried to Jehovah, being reluctant to throw their troublesome passenger overboard ; and when the storm abruptly ceased, it was so manifestly divine doing that " the men feared Jehovah exceedingly, and offered a sacrifice unto Jehovah, and made vows," This looks like true conversion, for prayer in an hour of peril does not always yield results after the peril is past. How wonderfully God works in order to turn men's hearts to Himself ! A storm at sea, an earthquake at midnight, and the quietness of a Gospel meeting all serve His purpose. He works as seems good in His perfect wisdom.

But this was not all in Jonah's day. When the prophet emerged from his watery tomb, and at last went to Nineveh, his preaching brought the whole population, from the king downward, low before God, and the threatened overthrow was averted. Alas, for the contrast when Jonah's Lord preached in Jerusalem ! No repentance was there, and He who will in due time sit upon the Great White Throne said, " the men of Nineveh shall rise in judgment with this generation, and shall condemn it : because they repented at the preaching of Jonah ; and behold, a greater than Jonah is here ! "

But as sure as Jonah's experience and preaching brought blessing and deliverance to many who were not of Israel, so our Lord's very real death and resurrection has brought salvation to millions everywhere. While still on earth, He maintained His position as Israel's Messiah, and refused the appeal of a woman of Tyre who addressed Him as Son of David ; and when He sent forth the twelve He bade them go not into the way of the Gentiles, nor enter into any city of the Samaritans, but go rather to the lost sheep of the house of Israel " (Matt. x. 5-6). But, risen from the dead, " He said unto them, Go ye into all the world, and preach the Gospel to every creature " (Mark xvi. 15). Israel's unbelief has caused " salvation to come unto the Gentiles, for to provoke them to jealousy " (Rom. xi. 11). The good news that Christ was delivered for our offences and raised again for our justification have reached our ears and our hearts, and brought us into peace with God (Rom. iv. 25 ; v. 1). " Blessed be God, our God ! " Let us spread abroad the good news with all holy earnestness.

(iv) *In the Fish's Belly*

THE path of obedience is the path of blessing. Peace and communion are found therein. Disobedience and self-will may seem to prosper for a time, but He who loves us infinitely will not suffer His own to continue thus. Disaster ensues from His all-wise chastening hand. In the midst of the storm, while others were praying, Jonah was sleeping. Conscience was being stifled by his self-will. How different with the Lord Jesus ! When the storm burst upon the Sea of Galilee, He slept peacefully in the stern of the vessel. As the perfect Man of faith, He could repose His weary head, assured of the Father's care. His sleep astonished the disciples as much as Jonah's sleep astonished the heathen mariners ; but how great the contrast between the fugitive prophet and the Man Christ Jesus !

When Jonah was cast out of the ship, a great fish swallowed him. " Prepared " does not mean specially created for the purpose. (although that would be an easy matter for the Maker " of the sea and the dry land ") ; it simply means that the fish was " appointed " for this service. The same word is thus rendered in Dan. i. 5 with reference to the food intended for Daniel and his companions. Much labour has been expended upon the great fish, as to what it was, and also upon Paul's thorn in the flesh as to its precise nature (2 Cor. 12) ; in both cases there are spiritual lessons of the highest importance, which such discussions tend to obscure. Jonah could certainly have said after his weird experience, " Before I was afflicted I went astray, but now have I kept Thy Word." (Psa. cxix. 67).

" Jonah prayed unto Jehovah his God out of the fish's belly." " His " God, be it noted ; for all sense of relationship was not lost (contrast 1 Sam. xv. 21 ; 1 Kings xvii. 12 ; xviii. 10). From many unlikely quarters prayer has ascended to God through the ages, but never anything quite like this. Prisons, caves, mountains, etc. have resounded with cries of anguish, but not the belly of a fish ! The chastened prophet owned the divine hand in what had befallen him. Chap. i. 15 says of the sailors, " *they* took up Jonah, and cast him forth into the sea " : but in Chap. ii. 3, Jonah says to God, *Thou* hast cast me into the deep, in the midst of the seas." He thus owned the divine hand, and humbled himself under it. He put in practice 1 Pet. v. 6-7 several centuries before the verses were penned. He was thus in the way of recovery. Deliverance can only come to souls in distress when the hand of God is acknowledged. Jonah, although in the belly of the fish, looked in faith towards God's holy temple, and he was sure that He who dwelt therein would hearken to his cry. " When my soul fainted within me, I remembered Jehovah : and my prayer came in unto Thee, into Thy holy temple " (chap. ii. 7). This is very beautiful, as showing that even when a saint gets into a backsliding condition he knows to Whom to turn in his trouble, and is confident that God will not forsake him.

The prophet's reference to the temple is remarkable in another way. Jehovah's temple stood in Jerusalem, and Jonah belonged by birth to the revolted ten tribes who had turned away from God's centre, and who were identified with idolatrous sanctuaries in Bethel and Dan. (1 Kings xii. 25-33 ; Amos vii. 13). Nevertheless, in spite of the religious confusion which disgraced Jehovah's land in his time, Jonah's heart turned towards the centre which was divinely established in happier days. To Solomon Jehovah said at the dedication of the temple, " Mine eyes and Mine heart shall be there perpetually " (1 Kings ix. 3). The glory-cloud still remained there, and thither the hearts of the faithful ever turned, wherever might be their abode. It was in this spirit Elijah set up an altar of twelve stones, although Carmel was in the territory of the ten tribes (1 Kings xviii. 31). God's principles, and the thoughts of His heart towards His people although in grievous failure, influenced both Elijah and Jonah.

In like manner, souls who to-day are taught of God maintain, " there is one Body and one Spirit " (Eph. iv. 4) and firmly refuse to recognize any other religious unity of any kind whatsoever ; and for His saints now God's centre is not a material structure, but the name of the Lord Jesus (Matt. xviii. 29). Do our hearts respond to this ?

Jonah's prayer in his second chapter is largely made up of quotations from the Psalms. His mind was evidently saturated with the written Word. Is this true of us also ? It was not a day of pocket Bibles, nor indeed were the Scriptures all yet written ; but if Jonah was unable to read in his strange prison, he could feed upon the Word already learned and stored up in his mind and heart. Let us not be behind him in this. The whole revelation of God is in our hands, containing wonderful counsels of grace and glory unknown in Old Testament dispensations ; shall we not seek to possess the whole in our inmost souls, so that if ever our Bibles are torn from us, we shall still have that which will nourish and sustain our faith ?

Meditation upon the Psalms, and the deliverances wrought for the writers, gave Jonah confidence. In his apparently hopeless condition he expressed his confidence in God-given terms. He was sure of deliverance ! He was persuaded that he would once more worship in the house of Jehovah ! " Salvation is of Jehovah," was his triumphant finish !

The work was done ; the lesson had been learned ; pride and self-will had received a heavy blow ; the prophet was at the end of his resources ; and his hope was in God alone. Every sinner has to learn this when he first draws near to God ; and the erring saint has to come back to it whenever he goes astray.

(v) *Grace to the Fallen*

THE words of the poet are certainly true, and we frequently sing them with real delight—

> " *To those who fall how kind Thou art,*
> *How good to those who seek.*"

The proof of this is found in both Old and New Testaments. When Elijah fled from the post of duty, terrified by Jezebel's threat, an angel was sent from heaven to prepare for him a fire and a breakfast (1 Kings xix.). Nothing like this happened while he walked in the path of obedience. At Cherith ravens were employed to supply his need, and that for a long period. But when he was all wrong with God he was granted special angelic service. The heavenly messenger apparently remained by him while he ate and drank and slept, and then a second time he urged him to eat more, adding compassionately, " because the journey is too great for thee." Yet the journey should never have been undertaken ! All this was divinely intended as a proof to the fugitive prophet that God had not forgotten him, spite of his break-down in service. What a God is ours !

Again, when Peter denied his Lord so painfully (after solemn warning) Luke tells us " the Lord turned and looked upon Peter " (ch. xxii. 61). That tender glance broke his heart, and " Peter went out and wept bitterly." After the Lord's resurrection, an angel bade the women (by divine authority, assuredly), " go your way, tell His disciples, and Peter, that He goeth before you into Galilee " (Mark xvi. 7). This touching introduction of Peter's name was intended to assure him that his Lord had not cast him off, notwithstanding his great sin. This was followed by a private conversation with the fallen Apostle, which put everything right (Luke xxiv. 34). Accordingly, when the Holy Spirit came at Pentecost, Peter was able to stand boldly and testify to the resurrection of his Lord, with mighty results (Acts ii. 41).

Jonah, when imprisoned within the fish, said, " I am cast out of Thy sight " (Jonah ii. 4). Surely he had no ground for complaint in this respect, seeing that he fled to Tarshish expressly to get away from the presence of Jehovah ! He even told the shipmen that this was the meaning of his voyage in their vessel (chap. i. 3, 10). Possibly Jonah familiar as he was with the Book of Psalms, had in mind David's words in Psa. xxxi. 22, " I am cut off from before Thine eyes," but David said this in haste ! We must quote the whole verse : " I said in my haste, I am cut off from before Thine eyes : nevertheless Thou heardest the voice of my supplications when I cried unto Thee." Oh, that precious " nevertheless " ! It is not the way of our God to cast off His saints, however deeply they may fail ; but He is always willing to hear the voice of their supplications when they cry. But let us beware of speaking in haste. Such utterances are seldom wise. Peter on the holy mount spake " not knowing what he said " (Luke ix. 33). There is " a time to keep silence " as well as " a time to speak " (Eccles. iii. 7).

Our brethren are not always as merciful in their dealings with us as our gracious God. When David was given the choice of three forms of chastisement after his proud blunder in numbering the people without reference to God, he said, " I am in a great strait : let me fall now into the hand of Jehovah ; for very great are His mercies ; but let me not fall into the hand of man " (1 Chron. xxi. 13). The " hired razor " can be very cruel (Isa. vii. 20) ; and was not David himself unnecessarily cruel when he cut the Ammonites " with saws and with harrows of iron, and with axes " ? " Even so dealt David with *all the cities* of the children of Ammon " (1 Chron. xx. 3).

Even after the Day of Pentecost, when the Assembly of God had come into being, with the Holy Spirit dwelling therein, and when the fulness of divine grace was being proclaimed as never before in the world's history, Paul had to admonish the Corinthian brethren to seek out, and forgive and comfort the man they had been obliged to put away for grievous sin. First, they were careless and indifferent to the evil ; then after they had been roused to action, they were disposed to have done with the man for ever. But he was repentant, and must not be " swallowed up with over-much sorrow." (2 Cor. ii. 6, 8). " I beseech you," says the Apostle, " that ye would confirm your love toward him." When shall we learn these lessons of divine grace towards the erring ? The merciless tyrant of Matt. xviii. 28-34 was meant to be a warning to all who bear the name of the Lord Jesus, and that to the end.

Jonah came up from the depths of the sea humbled and chastened. Scarcely *broken*, for the concluding chapter of his book shows that he still had much to learn. But he had experienced the power of God to lay low those who rise up against His will, and he was also assured that, come what may, God will never cast off His own. Jonah was one of the earliest of the prophets whose writings have come down to us ; but from his short book we may learn that God chastens His messengers as well as those to whom He sends them, but with a heart full of mercy which only seeks the blessing of its objects. May the messengers of God in this Gospel dispensation walk humbly before Him, and not misrepresent His character by ways of disobedience. Those who demand obedience from others should be models of obedience themselves. Moses was sharply dealt with by Jehovah because he had neglected to circumcise his son (Exod. iv. 24-25). He had apparently yielded to his wife in the matter ; but until this was put right, Moses could not consistently summon Pharaoh to be obedient to the divine commands. The lesson for us is the more important when we remember that circumcision signifies the judgment of the flesh. Only those who have learned to mortify their members which are upon the earth (Col. iii. 5) are competent to stand forth as witnesses for a holy God.

Listen to the words of the Lord Jesus, " if any will do His will, he shall know of the doctrine " (John vii. 17) " I came down from heaven, not to do Mine own will, but the will of Him that sent Me" (John vi. 38).

(vi) *The Second Commission*

WE need not suppose that the great fish remained stationary during the three days and three nights of Jonah's imprisonment ; but whatever may have been its movements, the eye of the Creator was upon it, and it was guided to drop the prophet just where Jehovah wanted him. The fish might have deposited him in Italy or Greece ; more probably it was in the land of Israel that Jonah set foot upon dry ground again. The obedience of the humblest creatures, as recorded in Scripture, is deeply instructive. The Lord Jesus when on earth wanted a fish which possessed a shekel, and that particular fish, and no other, caught at Peter's hook (Matt. xvii. 27). The colt upon which never man sat—an untamed novice for work—obediently carried the Lord through the streets of Jerusalem, although surrounded by a shouting multitude (Matt. xxi. 7). It might not have been wise for either reader or writer to mount that colt ! In like manner, the Mediterranean Sea monster was at the appointed place when Jonah was cast out of the ship ; it took care of him for the divinely appointed period ; and then released him in God's time, and in the place where God required him. Alas, that man, the most gifted of all earthly creatures, should be the arch-rebel of this planet ! The revolt of its head has involved the whole creation in groans and travail throughout the ages, which will only end at " the manifestation of the sons of God " (Rom. viii. 19-22).

Once more Jonah was commissioned by Jehovah to go to Nineveh (chap. iii. 1). Similarly, Peter, when restored from backsliding, was divinely appointed to carry a great message from God to men (Acts ii.). Jonah knew not what his message was to be when he set out. He proceeded " under sealed orders," as men say. " Arise, go unto Nineveh, that great city, and preach unto it the preaching that I bid thee." The spirit of obedience having returned to him (at least in measure) Jonah did not venture to reason with his Lord, after the manner of Ananias in Damascus when told to call upon Saul of Tarsus (Acts ix. 13, 14) ; but he " arose and went according to the word of Jehovah." This is as it should be, and it reminds us of Elijah when told to go and hide himself by the brook Cherith, " He went and did according to the word of Jehovah " (1 Kings xvii. 5).

This is the line that is proper for us all. The Apostle, when referring to his own movements, burst into praise thus : " thanks be unto God who always leadeth us in triumph in Christ (see R.V.), and maketh manifest the savour of His knowledge by us in every place " (2 Cor. ii. 14). He felt like a captive in a triumphal procession (such as the Romans were accustomed to give successful Generals on their return from the wars) ; but it mattered nothing to him where God led him—Troas, Corinth or elsewhere—so long as the will of God was carried out, and the savour of Christ was spread abroad. This made his life a great spiritual success.

Abraham's servant furnishes us also with a lovely example in Gen. xxiv. He went abroad in the spirit of prayer to seek a wife for his master's son. Having found the right person, he bowed his head, and worshipped Jehovah, saying, " I being in the way, Jehovah led me."

The only perfect servant and messenger was the Lord Jesus. When the anxious sisters sent from Bethany to tell Him, " Lord, behold, he whom Thou lovest is sick " ; the Evangelist records, " when He heard therefore that he was sick, He abode two days still in the same place where He was." Why the delay ? Because He had as yet no word from the Father ; but when the word came, even the warnings of His disciples that trouble awaited Him in Judea, could not hold Him back. (John xi.).

We are only of use to God when we are just were He wants us. He knows the right country in which we should serve, and the right town, and the right time. Office, factory, workshop or home— wherever it may be, if that is His place for us, there only can we be spiritually useful. And even when we are in the right place, we need the Spirit's guidance every hour as to what we should do or say. Simple lessons indeed ; but not necessarily learned and practiced by us.

When Jonah set out for Nineveh " according to the word of Jehovah," it is to be feared that there was some uneasiness in his mind as to the real object of his mission. Jehovah's new charge

mention of His judgment ; and they humbled themselves before
Him.   Jer. xviii. 7-10, as we have already seen, lays down the
principles of God's dealing with nations. His eye sees their doings,
and He visits them from time to time in His wrath, but is always
prepared to show mercy. God's government must not be confounded with His grace. Such respite as the Ninevites experienced is not
the same thing as the eternal forgiveness of sins proclaimed to men
everywhere in the Gospel message (Acts xiii. 38-39). We shall not
necessarily meet the whole population of Nineveh in Heaven because
of the repentance described in Jonah iii. 10 ; although it is not
unlikely that some individuals (possibly many) found eternal
blessing as the result of the great alarm.

At the present crisis the nations of the earth are suffering as
never before. He who sits upon the throne judging righteously is
displeased with them all, but if any nation (if only one) would face up
to its own condition in His sight, and acknowledge its manifold
transgressions and its long contempt for things divine, He would
forgive, and peace and quietness would return.   Mutual recrimina-
tions lead nowhere. To nations disposed to accuse and destroy their
neighbours, the prophet Obed's words in 2 Chron. xxviii. 9-11 may
well have a voice. When the victorious ten-tribe army brought
back 200,000 Jewish captives, the prophet met them boldly, saying,
" Behold because Jehovah God of your fathers was wrath with
Judah, He hath delivered them into your hand, and ye have slain
them in a rage that reacheth up unto heaven. And now ye purpose
to keep under the children of Judah and Jerusalem for bondmen
and bondwomen unto you ; but are there not with you, even with
you, sins against Jehovah your God ? "

(ix) *A Strange Dove*

IT is not only Divine names that have meanings ; there is also
meaning in human names at least in Scripture history. Sometimes they were expressive of the faith of those who conferred
them ; Eve, Noah, and Joseph are examples of this. Sometimes
new names were given as marks of lordship or proprietorship. Thus
Pharaoh renamed Joseph (Gen. xli. 45) ; Nebuchadnezzar did the
same to Daniel and his friends (Dan. i. 7) ; and the Lord Jesus
granted the surname Cephas to Simon the fisherman (John i. 42).
And what shall we say of the Saviour's own name and the meaning
of it ? " Thou shalt call His name Jesus (Jehovah the Saviour) ;

for He shall save His people from their sins " (Matt. i. 21).

Jonah means " dove." What was in the minds of his parents when they named him is not recorded ; but the fact reminds us that it was in a bodily form like a dove the Holy Spirit descended upon the man Christ Jesus (Luke iii. 22). This lovely emblem of purity, gentleness, and peace perfectly suited Him upon whom it came. But Jonah ! Where do we discover anything dove-like in his ways and words relative to the people of Nineveh ? Surely his cruel talons are suggestive of a very different bird !

We cannot help contrasting our prophet with Joses the Levite of Acts iv. 36-37. So kindly were his deeds, and so gracious was his ministry, that the Apostles surnamed him Barnabas which being interpreted, means " son of consolation." Barnabas deserved his name before he received it ; Jonah received a sweetly suggestive name that he never seems to have deserved at all !

Nineveh repented ; king, nobles, and people fell low together at the feet of their justly indignant Creator. Heaven was thus filled with rejoicing, as the Lord teaches us in Luke xv. But while heaven rejoiced, it displeased Jonah exceedingly, and he was very angry " (Jonah iv. 1). Alas, what is man ! What an exposure of the narrow- ness and selfishness of the human heart, even in a divinely chosen and specially favoured servant of Jehovah ! He would have pre- ferred the whole population of a vast city to perish than that his own reputation as a prophet should suffer ! He was amazed that he should have gone through the streets of Nineveh denouncing judgment within forty days, and then find the divine sentence withdrawn ! Yet why should God have given forty days notice, unless He desired to give time for repentance ? Does not Peter tell us that He is long-suffering to usward, not willing that any should perish, but that all should come to repentance " ? (2 Peter iii. 9). Did He not say, long before Peter's day, " I have no pleasure in the death of him that dieth, saith the Lord God ; therefore turn your- selves and live ye." (Ezek. xviii. 32). Even ecclesiastical Jezebel (Popery), the foulest evil upon which the eye of a holy God ever rested, has had space given her to repent of her fornication (Rev. ii. 21). Had Jehovah dealt with Jonah's own nation as he would have liked Him to deal with Nineveh, not an Israelite of any tribe would be found on earth today. Jonah's behaviour reminds us of the churlish elder son of Luke xv. 25 who " was angry and would not go in," because the father was lavishing grace upon a returning sinner. Where should we have been—reader and writer alike—if the God against whom we have all sinned were like some of His poor faulty servants

The disappointed prophet—by no means a friend or neighbour (at least for the time being) of the God who delights in mercy (Luke xv. 7)—prayed that he might be allowed to die. If death was so desirable, pity that he ever asked to be released from the fish's belly ! Elijah also once asked that he might die, because his testimony was not prospering as he expected (1 Kings xix. 4). Happily God intended for him a triumphant translation, without passing through death at all. A similar wonderful departure is the proper hope of all Christians to-day.

Although as wrong as he could be spiritually when he prayed his peevish prayer, Jonah had not lost all sense of his true relationship with God. Thus he addressed Him as " Jehovah," and said, " I pray Thee, O Jehovah, was not this my saying, when I was yet in my country ? Therefore I fled before unto Tarshish : for I knew that Thou art a gracious God, and merciful, slow to anger, and of great kindness, and repentest Thee of the evil ? " If he really knew all these delightful things about God, it should have been his joy to proclaim them to sinners everywhere. We know God more intimately still. The cross of Calvary has revealed grace and mercy such as Jonah could not have imagined. Is it our joy to proclaim it to young and old ? If we are to be successful in our testimony, our hearts must be in tune with the great compassionate heart of God. We must develop a yearning over the perishing, and it should be our prayer and labour that we may " by all means save some " (1 Cor. ix. 22).

Now mark the contrast between Jonah and the servant of Matt. xxv. 24. The latter looked his Lord in the face and said, " Lord, I know that Thou art a hard man, reaping where Thou hast not sown, and gathering where Thou hast not strawed." But Jonah said, " I knew that Thou art a gracious God, and merciful." Is there anything so perverse and contradictory as the heart of man ? He of Matt. xxv. charged his Lord with being hard and unreasonable ; and Jonah complained that He was too good ! We are reminded of the children in the market-place of whom the Lord spoke in Luke xi. 32. Neither John the Baptist nor the Lord Jesus suited their carnal taste. John was too austere, standing aloof from the people, and Jesus was over gracious, mixing too freely with all sorts and conditions seemingly giving the preference to publicans and sinners. " But wisdom is justified of all her children." (Luke vii. 35). This means that wisdom's true children, i.e., all who have been born of God understand and approve wisdom's ways ; while the wise ones of earth expose their folly by their failure to understand what God is doing. Unhappy Jonah ! He was doubtless born of God, but He was utterly out of harmony with His great heart of mèrcy. His mercy to the Ninevites was therefore vexation to him, instead of delight. Let us not miss this serious lesson. The Lord's own disciples were slow to learn it (Matt. xiv. 15 ; 15-23) although His companions from day to day.

(x) *"On the East Side of the City"*

JEHOVAH, instead of sharply disciplining His refractory servant, graciously condescended to reason with him " Doest thou well to be angry ? " Oh, the contrast between our God, Sovereign in the universe, and the petty despots of earth ! Such peevish rebelliousness as Jonah manifested might have cost him his life at the hands of the latter. But God always seeks to win men's hearts, both in dealing with sinners ' without ' and with wayward saints ' within.'

The gracious question of Jonah iv. 4 was repeated in ver. 9. To the first enquiry the prophet appears to have made no answer but we have the astonishing statement " Jonah went out of the city and sat on the east side of the city, and there made him a booth, and sat under it in the shadow till he might see what would become of the city." What a picture ! A man who has been handled with the utmost grace by his God positively sitting down (making himself comfortable withal) in the hope that God would change His mind and destroy the city ! Thus would his vanity be gratified, and his reputation as a true prophet be maintained ! Wretched self-importance, almost without parallel in the history of the world !

Our thoughts travel to Another Prophet ' greater than Jonah ' and ' greater than Moses ' (Deut. xviii. 15) Who at a later date sat on a hillside overlooking a different city, guilty before God beyond any other if only because it had been for many centuries the most favoured. Our Lord's last approach to Jerusalem was from the east. He followed Joshua's route from across Jordan. Arrived at Jericho (Rahab's Descendant, be it remembered—Matt. i. 5), the city did not fall before Him as before Joshua, for He had " not come to destroy men's lives, but to save them ! " Blessing tracked His footsteps, as Zacchaeus and Bartimaeus will be able to testify eternally. Then as He descended the Mount of Olives, and the long loved, but grievously guilty Jerusalem came into view, tears filled

His eyes. " If thou hadst known even thou, at least in this thy day, the things which belong unto thy peace ! but now they are hid from thine eyes. For the days shall come upon thee, that thine enemies shall cast a trench about thee, and compass thee round, and keep thee in one every side and shall lay thee even with the ground and thy children within thee, and they shall not leave in thee one stone upon another ; because thou knowest not the time of thy visitation " (Luke xix. 41-44).

Lovely manifestation of tender feeling, and that on the part of the Judge of quick and dead ! He who wept over Jerusalem is the same august Person who said in Hosea's day " How shall I give thee up, Ephraim ? how shall I deliver thee up, Israel . . . Mine heart is turned within Me " (Hos. xi. 8). If judgment must need be, it was nevertheless painful to the divine heart to be constrained to execute it. Judgment is " His strange work " (Isa. xxviii. 11). To such gracious sentiments the heart of Jonah was a stranger. How is it with ourselves? As faithful witnesses for God, it is our duty to warn an evil world of the judgment appointed (woe unto us if we neglect to sound the warning !) but how do we do it ? Is it in the stern spirit of denunciation, or is it with trembling lips and compassionate hearts ? Are we unmindful of the fact that but for the infinite grace of God and the costly sacrifice of the Lord Jesus, we should ourselves be in the lake of fire ? May God preserve us from the spirit of Pharisaism as we proclaim the fearful things which are certainly coming upon the world of the ungodly.

Jehovah had not yet finished with Jonah. Accordingly He " prepared a gourd, and made it to come up over Jonah, that it might be a shadow over his head, to deliver him from his grief. So Jonah was exceedingly glad of the gourd." Again we say, what a God is ours ! Here we have a man who deserved severe chastisement, and whom God might justly have banished from His service for ever, granted special divine relief from the effects of his own bad temper. But this was not the end. The relief was short-lived, for God prepared a worm the next morning, which " smote the gourd that it withered." Job, after immeasurable losses—property, servants, children, etc.—" fell down upon the ground and worshipped. And said, 'Naked came I out of my mother's womb, and naked shall I return thither ; Jehovah gave, and Jehovah hath taken away ; blessed be the name of Jehovah'" (Job i. 20-21). And He who suffered more than either Jonah or Job, when all was painful around Him, said, " I thank Thee, O Father ; Lord of heaven and earth . . . even so, Father, for it seemeth good in

Thy sight " (Matt. xi. 25-20).

But Jonah was rebellious. Twice he tells us in his book that he prayed unto Jehovah ; in the fish's belly, and in the neighbourhood of Nineveh. The first was a genuine outpouring of the heart under the mighty hand of God, and it brought a speedy reply ; the second was a peevish outburst because his journey to Nineveh did not result as he expected. Twice the angry man said, " it is better for me to die that to live." It is true enough that any of us had better die than live if we are not willing to " show forth the excellencies of Him who hath called us out of darkness into His marvellous light " (1 Pet. ii. 9). A witness who misrepresents the character of Him who sends him is worse than useless in a needy world.

The worm by the will of God did his destructive work in the early morning. Then the sun waxed hot, and a sultry east wind arose. Poor Jonah was overwhelmed, and dared to say to his Lord, " I do well to be angry, even unto death." This drew forth Jehovah's final remonstrance : " thou hast had pity on the gourd, for the which thou hast not laboured, neither madest it grow : which came up in a night, and perished in a night : and should not I spare Nineveh, that great city, wherein are more than sixscore thousand persons that cannot discern between their right hand and their left hand ; and also much cattle ? "

The book thus closes abruptly. Jonah was left to answer the challenge as best he could, and the reader of to-day is left to answer it for himself. The God whom we know—blessedly revealed to us in Christ—could do no otherwise than spare a repentant city. But this did not suit the surly preacher. His personal dignity was at stake (at least so he judged), and he would prefer Nineveh to be destroyed, with its immense population of old and young, rather than his words should fall to the ground. He had pity on the gourd, a creature of a day, because it was of advantage to himself, but there was no pity in his heart for hundreds of thousands of precious souls. If Jonah wrote his book in later life, as seems probable, surely he blushed with shame as he penned its concluding chapter under the guidance of the Holy Spirit.

Let us not miss the lesson. Away with all pride and self-importance. Let us learn to say with Paul, " I am nothing " (2 Cor. xii. 11). The Apostle had learned the meaning of his baptism. He had with all simplicity of faith accepted the death of Christ as his own, and he willingly passed out of sight. His dignities and attainments he counted loss for Christ. It was henceforward his earnest expectation and hope that Christ might be magnified in his body, whether by life or by death. (Phil. i. 20).

" For me to live is Christ."

" Be ye therefore imitators of me, as I also am of Christ." (1 Cor. xi. 1.).

(xi) *"The Compassionate Creator"*

THE last verse of the Book of Jonah should be carefully considered, for it gives us a delightful insight into the heart of God as Creator. His love and compassion for perishing sinners is happily familiar to us. It has reached us in the Gospel message. The cross of Christ tells out, as nothing else could, God's earnest desire for the salvation of men, and His unwillingness that any should perish eternally. But Jonah iv. 11 is not quite as John iii. 16. In the latter passage we hear the voice of the Son of God speaking on earth ; but in the former it is the Creator who is speaking, and that in terms of remonstrance with His ungracious servant. " Should not I spare Nineveh that great city, wherein there are more than sixscore thousand persons ' that cannot discern between their right hand and their left hand ; and also much cattle ? " Thus God in His government of the earth took account of 120,000 helpless children in Nineveh, " and also much cattle " ; and it rejoiced Him that the repentance of the King and his people enabled Him to sheathe the sword of judgment, at least for the time being.

It is deplorable when the servants of God are not in sympathy with His dealings. When the Lord Jesus was on earth there were two occasions when the compassion of His heart specially went forth. In Matt. ix. 36 He felt for the people's spiritual need. The land was full of religious leaders, but the people were unfed. " When He saw the multitudes, He was moved with compassion, because they fainted, and were scattered abroad, as sheep having no shepherd." In Matt. xiv. 15 He was concerned about their temporal need. He " saw a great multitude, and was moved with compassion toward them." Thousands of hungry men, women, and children were around Him, with nothing obtainable in the wilderness. But His disciples did not share the distress of their Lord. Indeed, they urged Him to send the multitudes away, regardless of consequences. The pressure of the people annoyed them, and interfered with their comfort !

A great lesson is here ! We live and serve in the midst of a suffering creation, and the suffering increases with the growing violence of men ; but are our hearts really moved by the serious universal need ? God's heart yearns over the masses, young and old, but do our hearts yearn in sympathy with Him ? It is terribly possible to become formal and stereotyped in our service, and thus to serve out of harmony with the One who has sent us. Let us seek to keep near the heart of the God of infinite compassion.

One of Jonah's faults was his intense nationalism. He could rejoice in divine forbearance towards his own people, although deeply guilty, but he felt unable to rejoice in God's forbearance towards others. We are reminded of the Apostle's query in Rom. iii. 29 : " Is He the God of the Jews only ? Is He not also of the Gentiles ? " Note the answer : " Yea, of the Gentiles also, seeing God is one." "Neither is there respect of persons with Him." (Eph. vi. 9).

Paul loved his own nation, and longed for their blessing (Rom. xi. 1). At one moment of exceeding fervour he had even wished himself accursed from Christ for his fellow-countrymen (Rom. ix. 3). The self-sacrificing prayer of Moses in Exod. xxxii. 32, and the passing wish of Paul in Rom. ix. 3, were doubtless acceptable to God ; but in no circumstances can sinners be saved by the self-sacrifice of preachers.

But Paul did not love Israel only. His heart went out after the uncircumcised to the world's end. He delighted to preach Christ where He had never been named (Rom. xv. 20). He could scarcely have told out the largeness of divine grace more explicitly than in Rom. x. 12 : " there is no difference between the Jew and the Greek ; for the same Lord over all is rich unto all that call upon Him, for whosoever shall call upon the name of the Lord shall be saved." But the largeness of the Apostle's heart was bitterly resented by the Jewish people. When he addressed them from the stairs of the Castle in Jerusalem, they listened quietly until he quoted the Lord's words to him, " I will send thee far hence unto the Gentiles." Then their fury burst forth, and they cried, " Away with such a fellow from the earth : for it is not fit that he should live " (Acts xxii. 21-22). When detailing offences in 1 Thess. ii. 16, he solemnly concluded thus, " forbidding us to speak to the Gentiles that they might be saved, to fill up their sins alway : for the wrath is come upon them to the uttermost." National feeling could scarcely go further ; even the unwanted Gospel must not be published abroad !

The whole world is ablaze while these lines are being penned. God in His righteous government has let loose the wild beasts of the earth, and the havoc that is being wrought is incalculable. But has

God ceased to care for His creatures ? Is He not still the " King of nations ? " (Jer. x. 7). Does He not now, as always, " do according to His will in the army of heaven, and among the inhabitants of the earth ? " (Dan. iv. 35). His hand has gone forth against the guilty nations of all Continents because of their neglect of His word ; yea, because of their ever-increasing contempt for everything that is divine.

The heart of God yearns over men notwithstanding all. His interest is not confined to any one nation, nor to a group of nations. He never was in special relationship with any nation but Israel, and against Israel the " Lo-Ammi " sentence (" not My people ") went forth long years ago, and has not yet been recalled. But the compassionate Creator can never cease to care for the afflictions of His creatures, however wayward, and He would have His saints share His compassion. Isaiah was deeply distressed when obliged to utter judgment against Moab, the bitter enemy of his own people. " My heart shall cry out for Moab " (Isa. xv. 5). " My bowels shall sound like a harp for Moab, and my inward part for Kir-haresh " (Isa. xvi. 11). Similarly, when Babylon's doom came before him in prophetic vision, he cried out, " My loins are filled with pain : pangs are taken hold upon me, as the pangs of a woman that travaileth " (Isa. xxi. 4). Jeremiah also howled for Moab, " mine heart shall sound for Moab like pipes." (Jer. xlviii. 31-36).

Where do we stand with reference to such sentiments in this day of unparalleled devastation and sorrow ? The public Press, and also the " wireless " would fill our minds with national feeling if we were to allow ourselves to come under their influence. Against this, God's saints must be continually on their guard. The house of God (" whose house are we " Heb. iii. 6) was intended to be " a house of prayer for all nations " (Mark xi. 17 ; Isa. lvi. 7) ; and we are exhorted in 1 Tim. ii. to make supplications, prayers, inter-cession and giving of thanks for all men, irrespective of nationality, and for kings and for all that are in authority whether friendly or unfriendly. Only as we are able to rise to this shall we be really helpful to men in their calamities. The great distinguishing principle of Christianity should aid us in this. God is at this time (while Christ sits on high and the Holy Spirit is on earth) visiting the nations " to take out of them a people for His name " (Acts xv. 14). Con-sequently, we have brethren in every land, and if all these, conscious of their union with Christ the Head, were to cry to God with one accord, the relief to the nations, amongst whom we all live and serve, would be incalculable.

God's heart is full of compassion towards all ; shame on us if we feel otherwise.

(xii) "A Type of Israel"

IT has already been remarked that Jonah's book is prophetic in character although it contains no such predictive utterances such as are found in Isaiah, Ezekiel, etc. The Christ who was to come is clearly foreshadowed in Jonah's three days sojourn in the belly of the fish : and the history of Israel may be clearly perceived in the disobedience of the prophet and its results for himself and others.

It was a great honour for Jonah to be divinely selected to carry a message from God to Nineveh, the imposing capital of the greatest earthly power in his day. Jonah should have endeavoured to enter into Jehovah's thoughts and feelings in the matter, so that he might faithfully represent Him to the dark heathen. In this the prophet most miserably failed. In like manner, the nation of Israel was divinely chosen and separated to be God's channel of blessing to all the people of the earth. " Ye are My witnesses, saith Jehovah, and My servant whom I have chosen " (Isa. xliii. 10). The most cursory reader of the Old Testament cannot fail to see that Israel occupies the central place therein. About four centuries after the flood when all the newly-formed nations had gone into idolatry God called Abram and blessed him ; but this was with a view to universal blessing. " In thee shall all the families of the earth be blessed " (Gen. xii. 3). This word was confirmed and expanded after the offering up of Isaac : " Thy seed shall possess the gate of his enemies, and in thy seed shall all the nations of the earth be blessed " (Gen. xxii. 17-18).

It was never intended that this highly favoured stock should be exclusive. Their very sanctuary was to be " a house of prayer for all peoples " (Isa. lvi. 7). It does not appear that Israel was meant to be a *missionary* people, earnestly propagating what they knew of the one true God, but they were certainly meant to be a *model* people. Possessing laws that were perfect, having been received direct from Heaven, all their ways should have been well-pleasing to God, and a rebuke to the nations around them. But, alas, they were untrue to their privileged position of separation to God (which alone could have made them a blessing to the world) ; they copied the evil ways of their neighbours ; and so brought down upon themselves the stern censure : " the name of God is blasphemed among the nations through you " (Rom. ii. 24). It will be a great day for the world when Zech. viii. 23 becomes true " thus saith Jehovah of hosts : In those days ten men shall take hold out of all languages of the nations, even take hold of the skirt of him that is a Jew, saying, ' We will go with you : for we have heard that God is with you'."

As surely as the unfaithfulness of Jonah brought a storm upon the pagan mariners, so the unfaithfulness of Israel has brought sore trouble upon the nations in general as well as their own guilty heads. When Jehovah could no longer bear with the iniquity of the chosen people, He employed Nebuchadnezzar to chastise both them and all the nations around them. The whole system of nations, of which Israel was the divinely established centre, was broken up. Abraham's seed thus became a curse in the earth, not a blessing.

Jehovah's patience with both Jonah and his nation is arresting. How graciously did He plead with the perverse prophet ! And how graciously did He bear with the hypocrisy of the Jewish remnant from the days of Ezra to the coming of the Lord Jesus ! Even then, in full view of their hatred, He pleaded that the unfruitful fig-tree be granted one year more (Luke xiii. 6-9). But the further testimony of the Holy Spirit after our Lord's return to heaven was all in vain, and once more the people were cast out of their land, and flung amongst the nations. The casting forth of Jonah typifies this. The chosen people are now most unlovable and unloved of all, and the whole earth has been plunged into confusion and disaster by the terrible transgressions in which Israel has led the way.

But the outflow of God's grace is not checked by the sin of man ; thus, while Israel continues obdurate, the Holy Spirit is working amongst the Gentiles, gathering out from amongst them millions for heavenly blessing. All these will stand in relationship with Christ as His body and bride for ever. Israel's fall has become the riches of the world and their loss the riches of the Gentiles (Rom. xi. 12). While hundreds of thousands of people in Nineveh were rejoicing in the mercy of God, Jonah was displeased and angry. Similarly, when a number of Gentile believers in Antioch were filled with joy and the Holy Spirit, the Jews " were filled with envy, and spake against the things which were spoken by Paul, contradicting and blaspheming " (Acts xiii. 44-52).

A great and wonderful change is coming. Israel's blindness is not total ; when the fulness of the Gentiles is gathered in " all Israel shall be saved " (Rom. xi. 25-26). This means the believing remnant, " for they are not all Israel which are of Israel " (Rom.

c

ix. 7). Obstinate rebels will be purged out (Ezek. xx. 38). The restored nation will stand before the world as though risen from the dead. Ezekiel's vision of the valley of dry bones shows this (ch. xxxvii). Dan. xii. 2 (a passage frequently misunderstood) teaches the same thing. The physical dead are not in view ; the nation as such is meant. After centuries of degradation in the dust they will come upon the political stage once more. The believing remnant will enjoy eternal life (in earthly conditions) and the rebels will be consigned to shame and everlasting contempt. Jonah's reappearance after being " three days in the heart of the seas " is typical of this. The following Scriptures should also be read in this connection :—Rom. xi. 15 ; Hosea vi. 2. Being then in the enjoyment of mercy themselves, the people, unlike Jonah, will gladly dispense blessing to others. Psa. lxvii. gives us their joyous language in that great day. Note the words " *all* the nations ; " "*all* the ends of the earth ; " " *all* rejoicing and singing for joy." " O sing unto Jehovah a new song : sing unto Jehovah, all the ends of the earth " (Psa. xcvi. 1). Alas, Jonah was not in singing humour as he contemplated the goodness of God to the Ninevites !

The whole earth will be fully blessed at the appearance of the Lord Jesus ; and Israel, completely purged of the Jonah spirit, will rejoice in it. God will be known, not merely as Creator, but as the faithful covenant-keeping Jehovah. " I will be known in the eyes of many nations, and they shall know that I am Jehovah " (Ezek. xxxviii. 23). This blessed result was reached in the case of Jonah's ship-mates. They turned from their own empty deities, and they " offered a sacrifice unto Jehovah, and made vows " (Jonah i. 16).

When Israel, after ages of antagonism to God and His blessed ways, perceives how marvellously He has wrought, they will say with the Apostle, " O the depth of the riches both of the wisdom and knowledge of God ! how unsearchable are His judgments, and His ways past finding out ! " (Rom. xi. 33). In deplorable imitation of Joseph's brethren they have intended evil in all that they have done to Christ and to His saints ; but God in His perfect wisdom has turned it to good (Gen. 41. 20). He will be victorious at last over all the workings of the enemy ; and every purpose of His grace will reach glorious fulfilment.

Alas, that the book of Jonah should close with the prophet murmuring outside while within the city there was gladness and peace. In this he was *not* a type of his nation. In the coming age of universal blessing Israel will be the centre and heart of it all. With the long-rejected Christ honoured in their midst, the people will be happy themselves, and will be delighted to see everyone happy around them even to the uttermost parts of the earth.

May the God of all grace grant to us all true largeness of heart. Thus shall we understand and approve His ways and find pleasure and profit therein for our souls.

(xiii) *The Destruction of Nineveh*

THESE studies would scarcely be complete without some reference to the after history of Nineveh, the great city in which Jonah preached, with results that will never be forgotten. It was founded by Asshur not long after the flood, apparently as a rival to Nimrod's Babylon (Gen. x. 11). The latter was built on the Euphrates, and the former on the Tigris (otherwise Hiddekel), both rivers being branches of the river which watered the Garden of Eden (Gen. ii. 13, 14).

But where is Nineveh to-day ? Opposite the town of Mosul there are miles of ruins from which many objects of interest have been excavated, and which are now in the Museums of Europe and America. The city was taken and destroyed by the Medes in B.C. 625. There has been no effort to rebuild it since that time, and it is not the will of God that it should ever be rebuilt. Its destruction was predicted with much detail by Nahum—remarkably, a Galilean prophet, as was Jonah. Nahum's book was written about 100 years after Jonah's mission, and the ruin therein foretold was still another century ahead. Who told Nahum about the great disaster ? The very principle is largely discredited in our time ; but if God be God, it is as easy for Him to speak of the future as of the present. This was His challenge to the deities of the heathen : " Let them bring forth and show us what shall happen : let them show the former things, what they be, that we may consider them and know the latter end of them ; or declare us things to come " (Isa. xli. 22).

Nahum's book begins thus : " The burden of Nineveh." The word " burden " occurs a number of times in the books of the Old Testament prophets. It means a heavy message—a message of judgment, a message which tends to weigh down the soul of him who has to deliver it. Nineveh was the capital of the Kingdom of Assyria. It is the city rather than the Kingdom that is denounced in Nahum ; whereas in Isaiah the Kingdom is condemned, with no special mention of its capital. This distinction is important. In the wonderful ways of God Assyria is to be restored and blessed in the Kingdom age (Isa. ixx. 23-25), but its proud capital will never rise again. Why is this ? The reason is that Nineveh was singularly favoured by God in its day. He sent Jonah there on a special mission, and the whole population trembled at the preaching, and cried to God for mercy. It does not appear to have led the Ninevites to the knowledge of Jehovah, as the great storm led the sailors in Jonah's vessel ; but the merciful Creator does not despise national repentance at any time. What wonderful results might be seen to-day if any of the contending nations were to humble themselves before God ! In His righteous Government He is chastening many nations as we write, for all deserve it in a greater or lesser degree. What joy it would give to the hearts of those who know God could we hear that any King, President, or Premier has called upon his people to repent, and that all have humbly responded !

Nahum says that " God is jealous, and Jehovah avengeth : Jehovah avengeth, and is furious ; Jehovah will take vengeance on His adversaries and He reserveth wrath for His enemies ; " but he also says that " Jehovah is slow to anger," and that " Jehovah is good, a stronghold in the day of trouble : and He knoweth them that trust in Him " (Nah. i. 2, 3, 7).

God is indeed " slow to anger." The evil of the Canaanitish nations was great in Abraham's day ; but even so He held back their judgment 400 years, " for ; " said He " the iniquity of the Amorites is not yet full " (Gen. xv. 16). From Rahab's words to the spies we learn that the guilty nations were aware that God's executioners were on their way. She said, " I know that Jehovah hath given you the land, and your terror is fallen upon us, and that all the in- habitants of the land faint because of you " (Josh. ii. 9). They had heard of God's heavy hand upon Egypt, and of the destruction of Sihon and Og, yet their was no repentance on their part.

Nineveh was granted forty days respite, with blessed results ; but the people soon returned to their wicked ways. Hence Nah. iii. 1 : " Woe to the bloody city : it is full of lies and robbery." This, as we have already remarked, was about 100 years after Jonah's visit, and even then the execution of judgment was delayed another century. We have said that Nineveh will never rise again, but in contrast with this, Sodom and her daughter cities are to be divinely restored for Millennial blessing (Ezek. xvi. 55). Does this strike any reader as strange ? The explanation is that Nineveh was favoured with a special message from God and submitted to it ; but the generations that followed profited nothing by the fact, and returned to the old vomit. But Sodom was never favoured as Nineveh was. In Matt. xi. 25 we hear our Lord saying that it shall be more tolerable for the land of Sodom in the day of judgment than for Capernaum, which city was honoured by His presence, ministry, and miracles. Favour divinely granted but despised brings heavy judgment from God. In Luke xii. 47-48 the Lord distinguishes between those who know His will and do it not, and those who sin without knowing His will. He says : " Unto whosoever much is given, of him shall much be required: and to whom men have committed much, of him they will ask the more." What could be more equitable ? In the light of our Lord's words where do the people of Great Britain stand ? Where in all the earth has the Gospel been so fully preached and the Scriptures more abundantly circulated ? The responsibility of people so privileged is great, and judgment will be meted out accordingly.

It is said that the overflowing of the river facilitated the capture of Nineveh by the Medes. Naham ii. 6 seems to teach this. Assyria —the nation—is to be blessed ; but to the once favoured city of Nineveh God has said : " Jehovah hath given commandment that no more of thy seed be sown." Deeply solemn words ! Truly, " it is a fearful thing to fall into the hands of the living God " ! (Heb. x. 31).

Jonah's behaviour as Jehovah's witness to the wicked city was most reprehensible. He was evidently puffed up with a sense of his own importance as he marched through the streets of Nineveh, the most famous city on earth at that time, and pronounced its impending overthrow. When the sentence was cancelled in answer to the people's repentance, Jonah should have rejoiced. Instead he felt piqued ! His dignity was touched ! Oh, the pettiness of poor flesh ! How ready it is to clothe itself with importance even in connection with the ministry of the word of God ! Had the prophet been right with God, he would have delighted to proclaim that He is a gracious God, merciful, slow to anger, and repenting Him the evil (Jonah iv. 2). Jonah's own nation, so persistently unfaithful has proved this repeatedly ; why should not others, less favoured, and therefore less guilty, also taste the mercy of a pardoning God ?

How blessed to be living in this Gospel age ! Let us feast our souls upon the words of our Lord Jesus : " God sent not His Son into the world to udge the world, but that the world through Him might be saved. He that believeth on Him is not judged : but he that believeth not is judged already, because he hath not believed

in the name of the Only Begotten Son of God " (John iii. 17-18).
" Verily, verily, I say unto you, he that heareth My word and
believeth Him that sent Me, hath everlasting life, and shall not come
into judgment, but is passed from death unto life " (John v. 24).

Part II.—" Balaam: His Words and Ways "

(i) *"Thou Hast Seen It"*

BALAAM and his evil doings are brought before us in eight books of Holy Scripture—five in the Old Testament and three in the New. This fact is sufficient to prove the seriousness of his activities. The last mention of Balaam (and Balak) is in the epistle to the Assembly in Pergamos (Rev. ii. 14). We learn from this that the wickedness of Balaam and Balak has been reproduced in the Christian circle. It is important therefore that every believer in the Lord Jesus should seek to understand what is involved therein.

Balaam appeared upon the scene in the closing days of Israel's forty years' journeyings in the wilderness. Aaron died at the age of 123 on the first day of the fifth month in the fortieth year. The people had reached their eighth encampment after Aaron's death when Balak and Balaam conspired against them (Num. xxxiii. 38-48). The question therefore arises, how did Moses get to know all that he has recorded in Num. xxii. 24 ? It is the story of things which took place behind the scenes as far as the people of God were concerned. No one in the camp could know of the negotiations between Moab and Amalek concerning an alliance against them ; nor could anyone know what was said and done in Balaam's house in distant Mesopotamia, and of the strange journey when even the ass rebuked its master for his folly. Also, seeing that Balaam's parables were all uttered from heights looking down upon the camp of Israel, none in the camp could be aware that anything was transpiring at all. Alas, the people were too much occupied with their murmurings to think of anything else ! How then did the inspired historian get the story of Balaam's doings and sayings which he has recorded with so much detail ? Moses must have got it all very quickly, for these things occurred during the last few weeks of his life. The answer to the question is simple ; Moses received the whole story by direct revelation from God. He knew, if His people did not, all that wicked men, urged on by Satan, were scheming against the people of His choice, and in His changeless

ove to them, notwithstanding their unfaithfulness from the beginning, He intervened and frustrated all the designs of the enemy.
He even constrained the mercenary soothsayer to say the very
opposite of all that he wished to say ! What a God is ours !

How little did the malicious conspirators think that God was
taking note of everything, and that the story of their doings would
be recorded by divine authority to be read by men in all succeeding
ages ! As little did the Roman officer Claudius Lysias imagine that
his lying letter to the governor Felix concerning Paul was noted and
preserved by God for insertion in His sacred Word ! (Acts xxiii. 25-
30). Let us never forget that all that we say and do concerning
persons we dislike, and which we hope they will never hear of, are
all observed and recorded by the all-seeing God. Every malicious
word and deed will have to be accounted for " in the day when God
shall judge the secrets of men by Jesus Christ " (Rom. ii. 16). Listen
to the words of Him who will sit upon the judgment-seat : " I say
unto you, that every idle word that men shall speak, they shall give
account thereof in the day of judgment " (Matt. xii. 36).

Direct divine revelation is the only explanation of other chapters
than Num. xxii. 24. Take, for example, the first two chapters of
the book of Genesis. There we are told of what God said and did
day after day during His great work of preparing the earth for the
habitation of man, and when the moment came for the man to be
created God said : ." Let us make man in our image, after our
likeness, and let them have dominion, etc." There was most certainly no scribe standing by to record all that the Creator did and
said during those wonderful days ; and we must have remained in
eternal ignorance of it all had not God been pleased to make the
whole matter a subject of divine revelation to the historian. Thus
we learn to trace everything to its true source—God. He who
questions either the possibility or the reality of divine revelation
has no claim whatever to be regarded as a Christian.

When Jehovah told Moses of the diabolical conspiracy against
Israel he might well have said in the language of the Psalmist :
" Thou hast seen it ; for Thou beholdest mischief and spite, to
requite it with Thy hand . break Thou the arm of the wicked; and
as for the evil man, seek out his wickedness till Thou find none"
(Psa. x. 14-15). When he told the people of the danger which had
threatened them, Moses said : " They hired against thee Balaam
the son of Beor of Pethor of Mesopotamia, to curse thee. Nevertheless Jehovah thy God would not hearken unto Balaam ; but
Jehovah thy God turned the curse into a blessing unto thee, because

Jehovah thy God loved thee " (Deu. xxiii. 4-5). Precious words—
" because Jehovah thy God loved thee ! " But how poor the
response from faithless human hearts !

(ii) *Balak's Fears*

WHEN Moses and the children of Israel sang their song of
triumph on the shores of the Red Sea, they said : " the
peoples shall hear and be afraid . . . the mighty men of
Moab, trembling shall take hold upon them . . . fear and dread
shall fall upon them" (Exod. xv. 14-16). This was fulfilled to the
letter when the King of Moab and his people beheld Jehovah's
pilgrim host encamped upon their frontiers forty years later. There
were in the camp of Israel 601,730 men able to carry arms ; with
women and children there were probably at least three million souls,
admittedly a vast company. Balak was alarmed ; the more so
because Israel had recently destroyed three military Powers which
had ventured to oppose their march. The King of Arad had gone
down ; likewise Sihon, King of Heshbon, and Og, King of Bashan
(Num. xxi). Sihon had some time previously waged a successful
war with Moab, and had annexed some of her territory ; how then
could Balak hope to stand up against a nation which had destroyed
his powerful neighbour ? When men are in trouble, the proper
thing is to turn to God in prayer. He is as truly interested in the
affairs of nations as in the difficulties and sorrows of individual
men and women ; but Balak knew nothing of God. If the rulers
of our own time would humbly spread out their troubles before God,
much grief and destruction would be spared. Jehoshaphat and
Hezekiah are two fine examples of kings turning humbly to God in
moments of national peril (2 Chron. xx. 2 Kings xix).

In reality Balak had nothing to fear. Jehovah had already said
to Moses : " Distress not the Moabites, neither contend with
them in battle ; for I will not give thee of their land in possession "
(Deut. ii. 9). Jehovah had in view a better portion for Israel than
the land of Moab. Moab typifies the comfortable, self-satisfied
man of the world—" at ease from his youth, settled on his lees "
(Jer. xlviii. 11). proud and arrogant in consequence (Isa. xvi. 6).
God's saints to-day need not envy such, for they have a better and
more enduring portion. " Blessed be the God and Father of our
Lord Jesus Christ, who hath blessed us with all spiritual blessings
in heavenly places in Christ " (Eph. i. 3). Asaph, when he got out

of communion with God, did envy the prosperity of the wicked ;
when he went into the sanctuary, and contemplated things there
with God, he recovered his spiritual equilibrium (Psa. lxxiii).

Knowing nothing of God, Balaam hastened to form alliances
with Midian and Ammon (Num. xxii. 4 ; Deut. xxiii. 3-4). Not
being satisfied that military power would suffice to withstand the
conquerors of Sihon and Og, he sent messengers to a noted soothsayer—Balaam the son of Beor, living in Mesopotamia. Israel's
victories were already being attributed to outsiders to divine
power. Thus Rahab said to the spies : " We have heard how
Jehovah dried up the water of the Red Sea for you, when ye came
out of Egypt, and what ye did to the two Kings of the Amorites
that were on the other side of Jordan, Sihon and Og, whom ye
utterly destroyed. And as soon as we heard these things our hearts
did melt " (Josh. ii. 10-11). In sending for Balaam Balak sought to
oppose the supernatural by the supernatural. The Mesopotamian
prophet was reputed to have influence with the invisible world—
" I know that he whom thou blessest is blessed, and he whom thou
cursest is cursed . . . Come now therefore, I pray thee, curse me
this people " (Num. xxii. 6).

This complex character had some knowledge of God—alas, no
heart knowledge ! He brought the name of the one true God into
his nefarious practises in order to give them an air of respectability.
Also, many persons would be more easily duped by his use of the
name of God. Balaam was what is now called a " Spiritualist." A
very misleading name really ; " Spiritist " or " Demonist " would
be more correct. Modern Spiritualists seem to be divided into two
classes : there are those who leave God quite out of their pretensions (which is at least honest) ; and there are also those who
call themselves " Christian Spiritualists." The latter class are
particularly dangerous ; for these are not Bible-reading days, and
many souls are easily led astray by the use of the word " Christian."
In quite a number of cases the clergy tamper with this great evil and
even recommend it as a useful adjunct to " preaching." The truth
is, there is no possible connection between Christianity and Spiritual-
ism. God in His word—notably in Deut. xviii. 9-14—unsparingly
condemns this iniquity in all its forms. It is apostasy—a turning
away from God and His revealed truth. It is intercourse with
demons, ruinous to all who practise it. The land of Canaan was
full of this when the hosts of Israel marched in, and they were
divinely charged to utterly exterminate it. Indeed, the prevalence
of this particular evil was one of the principal reasons why the

holy and righteous God could tolerate the seven Canaanitish nations no longer.

(iii) *The Invisible Powers of Evil*

THERE is no doubt whatever that we are surrounded by a vast world of spirits, some good, and some evil. The good are those who continue in their proper allegiance to the Creator ; the evil are those who are in revolt against Him, following the leadership of Satan. But both good and evil are deeply interested in the affairs of men ; the one delighting in their blessing, and the other seeking to compass their ruin.

There are three notices of the spirit-world in the epistle to the Ephesians which must detain us for a moment. In chap. i. 20-21 we have Christ's position in relation thereto. He is seated at God's " right hand in the heavenly places, far above all principality and power, and might and dominion." However mighty the spirit-forces in the universe may be, Christ is superior to them all, and all must yet acknowledge His Lordship. In chap. iii. 10 we are told " that now unto the principalities and powers in the heavenlies is made known through the Church the manifold wisdom of God." These are holy spirits, who observe with unselfish interest what God is doing for His redeemed, and they admire the wisdom of His ways therein. Peter says they desire to " look into " these things (1 Pet. i. 12). Then in chap. vi. 12 we learn that the Christian's present conflict is " against principalities, against powers, against the rulers of the darkness of this world, against wicked spirits in heavenly places " (see margin).

These spirit-forces are highly organised (we read of " chief princes " amongst them—Dan. x. 13) ; and their power is enormous. They act upon individuals to their ruin and they influence also the course of public affairs ; they are largely responsible for the disasters which come upon men from time to time. Kings and statesmen, however talented and well intentioned they may be, are helpless pawns in the hands of diabolical spirits, if they have not learned the need of absolute dependence upon God.

Let no-one misunderstand the foregoing. We are not referring to the spirits of departed men and women. These are quite unable to influence earthly affairs, even if they know anything at all about them, which is very doubtful. Our reference is to angelic beings, some good, and some evil, as before stated. Men have always had a desire to pierce the veil which separates the visible from the invisible. Such inquisitiveness is dangerous in the extreme, and those who indulge in it expose themselves to the tyranny of beings greatly their superiors in power and subtlety, who delight to allure souls down to eternal ruin.

It has pleased God, in His gracious instruction of His own saints to give us glimpses of what is going on in the invisible world. He wishes His own, who are set in testimony for Him here, to have some understanding of the terrible influences which are persistently working for the destruction of the human race. We are thus ourselves preserved from Satanic deception, and are able to warn others also. Daniel x. 1 ; xii. 4 ; 1 Kings xxii. 14-23 ; and Rev. xvi. 12-16 are scriptures which every Christian should carefully examine in this connection. In Dan. x. we find the prophet in prayer for three weeks concerning the future of the people of Israel. At the end of that period an angel came to him saying that he was sent off at once with the answer, " but," said he, " the prince of the kingdom of Persia withstood me one and twenty days " (ver. 13). Of whom is the angel speaking ? Not of a man, certainly ; for how could the Persian Sovereign hinder an angel coming from heaven with an answer to the prophet's prayer ? And would he be likely to know that the prophet had prayed at all ? It is a mighty spirit of whom the angel speaks, a spirit that interested itself for good or for evil in the politics of the Persian State. Then in ver. 20 we read : " now will I return to fight the prince of Persia : and when I am gone forth, lo, the prince of Grecia shall come." It is impossible to introduce men into such a passage. The angel is speaking of movements and counter movements in the spirit-world, resulting in conflicts here upon earth. If the angel's message be read through to the end (chap. xii. 4), we shall learn of many mischievous doings on the part of Kings and others, energised by Satan ; we shall also learn that Israel forms the centre of God's earthly ways, and that the archangel Michael has special charge of Israel's interests and that in due time he will act in power on their behalf. (Dan. xii. 1). In connection with this interesting angelic communication to Daniel, Zech. i. 7-11 ; iii. 1-5, and vi. 1-8 may well be carefully considered.

Turning now to 1 Kings xxii. 14-23. Ahab—Israel's wicked and wilful king—was disposed to go to war with Syria for the recovery of Ramoth-Gilead. His misguided ally, Jehoshophat King of Judah (pious, but weak) wished to know what Jehovah might have to say about the undertaking. In due course faithful Micaiah was brought out of prison, and in few words he described a scene in the heavenlies. Jehovah was seated on His throne surrounded by the host of heaven. His patience with Ahab being now exhausted, He called for a volunteer who would dispose the doomed man to go to war to his undoing. After much discussion, a spirit proposed to go down and put a lie in the mouths of all the King's prophets. " Go forth, and do so," said the great God. No words can adequately set forth the solemnity of this. Israel's war with Syria was thus arranged in the spirit-world, as many a war since. Blinded by Satan, Ahab paid no heed to what he heard. God's faithful witness was sent back to prison, and the King rode forth to his death.

Rev. xvi. 12-16 deals briefly with the last gathering of the nations for battle. The dread word " Armageddon " is found here. Spirit-forces are responsible for the world's final conflict. It will suffice to quote the passage " I saw three unclean spirits like frogs come out of the mouth of the dragon, and out of the mouth of the beast, and out of the mouth of the false prophet. They are the spirits of demons, working miracles, which go forth unto the kings of the whole earth, to gather them to the battle of the great day of God Almighty." The language is doubtless symbolic, but its meaning is too plain to be misunderstood. As the scriptures become more and more neglected and discredited (largely as the fruit of the so-called " Higher Criticism ") men will listen with increasing willing-ness to " seducing spirits, and doctrines of demons, speaking lies in hypocrisy " (1 Tim. iv. 1-2). Terrible result of the poison of unbelief injected by the serpent into the minds of Eve and Adam at the beginning ! (Gen. iii. 1).

One of the oldest of the Books of the Bible enlightens us as to Satan's malicious activity against individuals.

When various disasters came upon Job, he had no idea that he had been the subject of conversation in the heavens. Jehovah had observed his ways with much pleasure ; Satan also had observed him, but with malignant eyes. When Jehovah raised the question of Job with Satan, he was answered with the insinuation that Job only served Him for his own advantage. God therefore allowed the enemy to strip him bare of all that He had given him ; yet Job did not renounce his God. At a second conversation in the heavens, Satan urged that the trouble had not gone far enough, and if God would touch the patriarch's person He would see what manner of man he really was. We will not pursue the familiar subject further ; but when Job's friends, having heard of his troubles, came to visit him, and found him covered with boils, sitting in anguish upon an ash-heap, their words and also Job's show that none of them really understood the matter. But Job clave to his God, spite of His strange dealings with him, and in the end he was more richly blessed than ever.

The Scriptures that we have examined tell us a little of the hostility of Satan and his hosts to God and to men individually and collectively. A great day is coming, and it may be very near, when a mighty clash of spirit-forces will take place on high, resulting in the expulsion of Satan and his angels from the heavens, never to have a footing in those regions again. Then will be heard the shout of triumph from the glorified saints : " Now is come the salvation, and the strength, and the Kingdom of our God, and the power of His Christ ; for the accuser of our brethren is cast down, which accused them before our God day and night " (Rev. xii. 7-12).

Having some knowledge of these terrible forces of evil, Balaam was willing to be their tool for the destruction of God's people Israel, but Jehovah, who loved the people, frustrated him at every point, and from his lips there flowed not curses but blessings !

(iv) *To and From Mesopotamia*

" **M**ANY shall run to and fro " (Dan. xii. 4). Even since the expulsion from Eden man has been a restless being. He is never more restless than when he is in trouble, or when he thinks he sees trouble approaching. North, South, East, and West are searched for help, or for a way of escape. Thus, when Balak became alarmed by reason of the proximity of the people of Israel to his borders, he sent messengers to neighbouring kingdoms seeking alliances, and he also sent messengers to Mesopotamia to bring along the renowned soothsayer Balaam. He would have done better to get down before God, who never turns aside the supplications of those who feel their need of Him. In our own day we have seen statesmen flying thousands of miles at the risk of their lives to consult with flesh and blood concerning their anxieties. A day of fasting and prayer on the part of these statesmen would produce better results. Oh, the blindness which prefers flesh, with its notorious fickleness, to God with His well-known faithfulness to all who put their trust in Him ! (Isa. ii. 22).

Balak's messengers went to Mesopotamia " with the rewards of divination in their hands " (Num. xxii. 7). Knowing that the

false prophet " loved the wages of unrighteousness " (2 Pet. ii. 15).
Balak sought to make sure of him by sending " cash in advance ! "
But the treacherous deceiver introduced Jehovah's name into the
matter, and lodged the messengers for the night under the pretence of
seeking the mind of God. The business in hand was of immense
importance, for he was required to effect the ruin of a whole nation ;
did he therefore spend the night in prayer to God ? Nothing was
further from Balaam's thoughts. He simply went to bed ; and God,
who was watching all these movements with the deepest interest,
came to him with the challenge, " What men are these with thee ? "

Let us note the whole position carefully. The people of Jehovah,
who had been ungrateful and disobedient throughout their wilderness journey, were now in grave peril. They were not aware of it
and therefore did not make supplication to God. But Jehovah
Himself took the matter up, and there we are reminded of His
changeless favour. He loved the people, spite of all that they were,
and He would not allow the enemy to harm them. Oh, the comfort
of this thought for ourselves !

Was Balaam aware who it was that spoke to him that night ?
This is not certain when we remember that he was a man accustomed
to hearing voices from the invisible world. But whether or not he
understood at first that it was Israel's God who was dealing with
him, he replied quite frankly that Balak requested him to curse a
people who had come out of Egypt, of whom he was afraid. The
answer of God was in three short sentences. (1) " Thou shalt not
go with them." This should have sufficed to close the matter
absolutely. A man who really knew God would never raise the
question again. (2) " Thou shalt not curse the people." Therefore
however much his covetous heart might desire Balak's silver and
gold, he must not attempt to do what Balak desired. (3) " They
are blessed." A man who knew God would be assured that God
would never go back upon this. Here is the whole divine communication : " Thou shalt not go with them : thou shalt not curse
the people, for they are blessed ! " "And I cannot reverse it," said
Balaam later !

His words to his visitors next morning have a tinge of disappointment in them : " Jehovah refuseth to give me leave to go with
you." His heart was not in communion with God about His
people. Gladly would he have overwhelmed them in ruin for the
sake of reward ; but he was conscious of divine restraint.

When Balak's messengers returned to Moab, the King was not
disposed to let the matter rest. Accordingly he sent another

embassy, composed of persons greater in dignity than those he sent at first, and offered to increase the reward if only Balaam would come. Balaam said that if Balak would give him his house full of silver and gold he could not go beyond the word of Jehovah. This sounds well ; but he added " tarry ye also here this night, that I may know what Jehovah will say unto me more " (Num. xxii. 18-19). Such an attitude was sheer wickedness. Jehovah had already clearly stated His mind ; thus there was nothing about which to consult Him further. But Balaam was bent upon going, and he knew enough of God not to desire open conflict with Him (like Gamaliel in Acts v. 39) ; he would bend Jehovah to his self-will if possible ! Appalling thought ! Colossal ignorance of our God !

God spoke again to Balaam in the night, saying, " If the men have come to call thee, rise up and go with them ; but the word that I shall say unto thee, that shalt thou do." God would now deal with the fool according to his folly. He should go as he wished ; but God was determined to cover him with confusion, and bring great blessing for His own people out of these Satanic manoevres. The man's wicked attitude towards God concerning this matter calls to mind the behaviour of the Jewish captains in the days of Jeremiah when they were afraid of the Chaldeans. They requested the prophet to pray for them that they might have divine guidance concerning their path, when they had already made up their minds to go with their whole company to Egypt (Jer. xcii.). Let us beware of going before God at any time with our minds already made up. It is a serious affront to the Divine Majesty !

Balaam, having obtained permission from Jehovah, arose eagerly in the morning, saddled his ass, and set forth with Balak's messengers. He was not walking in the light, as the Lord Jesus in John ii. 9, when starting on a journey. Balaam walked in darkness, hoping that he was to have his own way, and reap a rich reward for his villany. His heart was not filled with divine affections, and longing to be used of God for the blessing of men. He had no message ; what he would be constrained to say when his eyes beheld the tribes of Israel he knew not. What a journey—a journey that will preach its lessons, and that will not be forgotten while the earth abides ! Never was Satan more determined to curse ; never was God more determined to bless ! Never had Satan a more willing servant ; never was a man more impotent than Balaam when the Almighty took him in hand ! How good to the soul to meditate upon the ways of our God !

(v) *"The Madness of the Prophet"*

OUR generally excellent Authorised Version is faulty in its rendering of 1 Tim. vi. 10. The apostle did *not* say, " the love of money is the root of all evil," for it is indisputable that many evils are sometimes found in persons who are not plagued with the love of money at all. The Revised Version gives the meaning more correctly : " the love of money is a root of all kinds of evil." From that pernicious root envy, lying, and murder (not to mention other sins) can easily spring. But the same hateful things can also come from other roots. Love of money was the ruin of Balaam, as of Judas Iscariot and many others. The Holy Spirit when commenting upon Balaam's doings fifteen centuries later said, " he loved the wages of unrighteousness ! (2 Pet. ii. 15).

So we picture the prophet setting out from Mesopotamia for Moab with Balak's silver and gold filling his soul's vision, utterly heartless as to the devastation and sorrow that he was to endeavour to bring upon an unoffending people in order to obtain his reward. The people of Israel had done him no wrong, and he had no direct quarrel with them ; yet he was willing to blast a whole nation—men. women, and children ! Nothing more horrible could well be imagined. No wonder we read that " God's anger was kindled because he went " (Num. xxii. 22).

A heavenly being stood in the way with a drawn sword in his hand. He is called " the angel of Jehovah." This was no mere servant. It is the same messenger who appeared to the wife of Manoah in Judges xiii and who said his name was " Wonderful." Both to her and to Balaam he spoke with divine authority. To Balaam He said : " I went out to withstand thee, because thy way is perverse before Me . . . Go with the men; but only the word that I shall speak unto thee, that thou shalt speak." The speaker was none other than He whom we know as the Lord Jesus Christ.

The ass saw the Angel, and turned aside from the threatening sword. Alas, that the beast should have more perception than a man made in the image of God ! " The ox knoweth his owner, and the ass his master's crib : but Israel doth not know, My people doth not consider" (Isa. i. 3). Such was Jehovah's complaint of the moral insensibility of the people to whom He had been more kind than to any other. The very cattle could put them to shame !

Balaam smote his ass three times. The Angel rebuked him for it, for every act of cruelty to animals is divinely noted.

When the sons of God are manifested in glory with the Firstborn, the groaning creation will be finally delivered (Rom. viii. 19-22). Meantime, " Jehovah opened the mouth of the ass " Let no-one doubt it. The Holy Spirit, who is the real Author of every book of Scripture, says so, not only in the book of Numbers, but in the much later second epistle of Peter. This answers every question to those who have learned to believe God. Why should not the ass speak ? He who gave speech to man can surely give speech to a beast at any moment if circumstances require it. " The iron did swim " (1 Kings vi. 6). " The sun stood still " (Josh x. 13). And, pray, why not ? " Is anything too hard for Jehovah ? " (Gen.xviii. 14). Bring Him into these matters, and all difficulties vanish. " None can stay His hand, or say unto Him, What doest Thou ? " (Dan. iv. 35).

"The dumb ass speaking with man's voice forbade the madness of the prophet." Madness indeed, to imagine that he could annul or change the declared purpose of Jehovah concerning His people ! Madness to suppose that a beneficent Creator would allow millions of souls to be destroyed in order that a spiritualistic practitioner might earn a fee ! But what madness are men not capable of who are ignorant of God ? Is the devastation of the earth in our own time evidence of wisdom or madness ? Had Balaam any heart-knowledge of God he would have refused to go a step further after his experience with the Angel. True, the Angel said, " Go with the men ; but only the word that I shall speak unto thee, that thou shalt speak." But he also said, " Behold, I went out to withstand thee, because the way thou walkest in is for ruin before Me " (Num. xxii. 32, Darby). After hearing all this, Balaam was clearly proceeding to his doom. His words " I have sinned " no more came from a divinely convicted conscience than the same words from the lips of self-willed Saul in 1 Sam. xv. 24.

In due course Balaam met Balak, and was rebuked by him for not coming when first invited. But it must have been with a more than doubtful mind that Balaam entered upon the sorry business for which he had been summoned from Mesopotamia. In some respects these two servants of the Devil foreshadowed the beast and the false prophet of the last days, who will with diabolical energy move earth and hell against the Israel of God for their destruction, but who will have no more success than the Balak and Balaam of long ago. Indeed they will be " cast alive into a lake of fire burning with brimstone " (Rev. xix. 20). Who is able to withstand God ?

(vi) *The Great Question*

G OD has a twofold controversy with Moab concerning the people of Israel : first, " because they met you not with bread and water in the way when ye came forth out of Egypt," and, second, " because they hired against thee Balaam the son of Beor of Pethor of Mesopotamia to curse thee " (Deut. xxiii. 4). We learn from this that sin can be negative as well as positive. He who neglects to do the will of God is as real a sinner as he who openly defies it. In Matt. xxv. the foolish virgins were shut out from the marriage feast because they neglected to obtain oil for their lamps ; the servant with the one talent was cast into outer darkness because he neglected to use his talent for the Lord, and the " goats " were sent away into eternal punishment because they neglected to show kindness to the King's messengers. Such neglect as is exposed in Matt. xxv. suggests contempt for the will of God—a very serious matter indeed. Samuel said to the people of Israel : " God forbid that I should sin against Jehovah in ceasing to pray for you " (1 Sam. xii. 23). It was evil therefore in the sight of God that Moab (and Ammon) did not meet His pilgrim people with bread and water when they were marching from Egypt to Canaan.

But these enemies went further. There was not mere neglect but also open hostility. Many centuries after Moses' day Jehovah said, " O My people, remember now what Balak King of Moab consulted, and what Balaam the son of Beor answered him from Shittim unto Gilgal, that ye may know the righteousness of Jehovah" (Micah vi. 5). A great question was thus raised by Balak and Balaam under the instigation of Satan against the people of Israel— a question which it is important we should understand, for it affects us intimately. Satan is as full of malignity against God's heavenly saints as against his earthly people. Israel was delivered from Egypt by the power of God, with promises of blessing in a divinely chosen land ringing in their ears ; their path, year by year, was marked by divine love and care ; the people were now on the threshold of the promised land ; and the moment had almost come for them to cross the Jordan and take possession. Satan, who had wrought havoc amongst them persistently during the wilderness years, now roused himself for a supreme effort against them, Balak and Balaam being his chosen instruments. He sought to deprive them of the promised blessings ; indeed, he desired their utter extermination. Had the great question been raised at the beginning of the forty years everyone would have expected

Jehovah to refuse the suggestion to destroy the people. Why deliver them from the taskmasters of Egypt, and why preserve them from the perils of the Red Sea if He was willing to destroy them ? But the question was not raised at the beginning of the forty years, but at the end. And what was the history of those years ? On Jehovah's part, goodness, faithfulness and patience ; but on the people's part unbelief, ingratitude and persistent disobedience ! Moses truly loved the people and sacrificed all his wordly prospects in order to serve them, but they broke his heart, and on one occasion they so provoked his spirit that he uttered words which deprived him of the land of his soul's deep desire (Isa. lvi. 32-33 ; Num.xx. 12 ; Deu. iv. 21-22). With such a record, could the people be cursed ? Could Jehovah be induced to cast Israel aside ? This was the question that was raised and answered in the plains of Moab.

We study this grave chapter in Israel's history with deep interest because it concerns us vitally. What have we been towards our God during the days of our pilgrimage ? We must all bow our heads with sadness and shame as we put this question to our hearts. But can our shortcomings affect God's counsels of grace concerning us ? Will He cease to love us, erase our names from the book of life, and fling us back to where He found us ? Blessed be His holy name, NO ! He chose us in Christ before the foundation of the world that we should be holy and without blame before Him in love ; He has taken us into favour in the Beloved ; He has washed, sanctified, and justified us ; and has sealed and anointed us with the Holy Spirit (Eph. i. 3-6 ; 1 Cor. vi. 11 ; 2 Cor. i. 21-22). All this must stand for ever, for God is faithful, whatever His people may be. In His righteous government He may chasten us even as He chastened Israel of old, but He will never abandon His counsels of grace. " The gifts and calling of God are without repentance " (Rom. xi. 29). Listen to Moses in Deut. xxiii. 5 : " Jehovah thy God would not hearken unto Balaam, but Jehovah thy God turned the curse into a blessing unto thee, because Jehovah thy God loved thee;" similarly, all our blessings are secured in the risen Christ, and the Father loves us as He loves Him.

It suits the arch-hypocrite of the universe, Satan, sometimes to make a stand for righteousness. Can it be consistent with the divine character that an unfaithful people should still be loved and blessed ? In Zech. iii. the prophet was shown in a vision Satan resisting Joshua as representative of the nation of Israel. He would fain have the man in filthy garments flung into the fire as wholly unsuitable for the presence of God. But he was divinely rebuked ! Satan before he fell held high office in the creation of God. There is a veiled allusion to him in Ezek. xxviii. 11-17. We quote verse 14 : " thou art the anointed cherub that covereth, and I have set thee so : thou wast upon the holy mountain of God ; thou hast walked up and down in the midst of the stones of fire." These words make it apparent that Satan's office was to guard the interests of the throne of God. In his hypocrisy even now he " transforms himself into an angel of light" and his servants into "ministers of righteousness " (2 Cor. xi. 14-15). Evil spirits are not always unclean (Mark v. 2) ; they can be sanctimonious and Pharisaical when it suits them (1 Tim. iv. 1-3). They could even by the lips of men charge the Lord Jesus with Sabbath-breaking, blasphemy, and sedition ! They could affect to be shocked at the ways and words of God's Holy One !

As we read the book of Numbers it is delightful to discover that the efforts of wicked men and of Satan caused God to give forth, by the unwilling lips of Balaam, some of the most marvellous outpourings of grace and blessing concerning His people that we find anywhere in Scripture. In explanation of this we should glance back at Num. xxi. 8-9. The uplifted serpent was a type of the uplifted Son of Man as we learn from His own blessed lips in John iii. 14. This suggests God's utter rejection of flesh as hopelessly evil in His sight. Nothing that proceeds from the first man can be acceptable to Him. The sinner needs not only forgiveness for the sins which he has committed ; he needs also a new and divine life. This is what Nicodemus was told at the midnight talk in Jerusalem. A truly humiliating lesson for us all to learn ! The root is bad as well as the fruit ; the life as well as its evil manifestations. Life for man is only found in Him who upon Calvary's tree bore the judgment of God against all that we were and against all that we have done. He lives now in resurrection power, and every believer is entitled to say " the life that I now live in the flesh (i.e. in the body) I live by the faith of the Son of God, who loved me, and gave Himself for me " (Gal. ii. 20.).

In the uplifted serpent Jehovah (typically) put out of sight all the inbred evil of the people of His choice ; how then could He cancel all His purposes of grace, and cast them away from His presence ? The devices of the enemy turned to his own confusion, and furnished the God of all grace with an opportunity to set forth more clearly and fully than ever the great thoughts of His heart.

Let us read again Micah vi. 5. " O My people, remember now what Balak King of Moab consulted, and what Balaam the son of

Beor answered him from Shittim unto Gilgal; that ye may know the righteousness of Jehovah." This is a truly remarkable passage when we consider the places which are named therein. " Shittm " was on the wilderness side of the Jordan, but " Gilgal " was inside the promised land. Thus Jehovah's answer to the enemy was in deeds as well as in words. His *words* were uttered in Shittim (and very full and wonderful they were); His *deeds* were witnessed in Gilgal, where the people of Israel, after their miraculous crossing of the Jordan, pitched their camp, and from which they went forth conquering and to conquer. Most blessedly therefore did Jehovah display His righteousness in the fulfilment of His gracious word to His people. But how quickly they forgot His works, and ceased to sound forth His praise !

(vii) *God's Sanctified People*

BALAK met Balaam at the frontier of his kingdom. Neither king nor prophet were in good humour. Balak was affronted because Balaam had not readily responded to his requirements ; and Balaam had the feeling that he was under restraint, and that matters would not develop as Balak and himself desired. Balak first took his visitor to Kirjath Huzoth, and there he offered oxen and sheep in the presence of Balaam and of the princes who had fetched him from Mesopotamia. We may perhaps regard this as a kind of official welcome. To whom Balak offered his sacrifices we are not told ; certainly the one true God had no place in his esteem. (Num. xxii. 36-41).

On the following day the real business commenced. " Balak took Balaam, and brought him up into the high places of Baal, that thence he might see the utmost part of the people." This is the first mention of Baal in the Word of God. It was the chief male deity of the Phoenicians and the Canaanites, Ashtoreth being the chief female deity. (Sorrowful words to write !). This form of idolatory obtained a footing in Israel in the days of the judges ; it was cast out in the time of Samuel (1 Sam. vii. 3-6) ; it became firmly established in the kingdom of the ten tribes in the reign of Ahab ; and Jezebel's daughter Athaliah introduced it into the Kingdom of Judah. This great evil was one of the causes of the expulsion of the whole twelve tribes from the land of promise.

Balak's object in conducting Balaam to the high places of Baal was that probably such a stronghold of his false worship would be favourable to the business in hand. Surely at such a spot Baal would help him ! But he reckoned without God, and in a short time he was compelled to listen to the Gospel of God from the Devil's own platform ! What discomfiture ! Balaam took up the matter and asked Balak to build seven altars, and prepare for him seven oxen and seven rams. This wicked man probably had some knowledge of the sacrificial system which Jehovah had instituted in Israel. He knew that burnt-offerings were acceptable to Him ; but did he really imagine that the presentation of sacrifices from such a man as himself would be so agreeable to Jehovah that after all He would allow him to have his own way, and curse the people ? His blindness and ignorance in offering burnt-offerings at such a moment was remarkable. But whatever the oxen and rams on the altars meant to Balaam they suggested Christ to God ; and when Christ is before Him in the perfection of His great sacrificial work, what can He do but bless His people ? Balaam understood nothing of this. He was as blind as the wicked men who put the blessed Son of God upon the cross of Calvary. There was an aspect to that cross of which they knew nothing. Little did they imagine that God would bring vast blessing out of their appalling deed !

As the smoke of the sacrifices ascended, " Balaam said unto Balak, stand by the burnt-offering and I will go ; peradventure Jehovah will come to meet me : and whatsoever He sheweth me I will tell thee " (Num. xxiii. 3). Such a speech was an exposure of the man. Why the word " peradventure " ? Did God ever refuse to meet any soul that sincerely sought Him ? Why this language of uncertainty ? It was pious cant. When he turned aside to " a bare height " Balaam had no wish whatever to meet Jehovah. His one desire was that Jehovah would let him alone, that he might do what Balak wished, and so earn his reward. Num. xxiv. 1 tells us definitely that he went " to seek for enchantments," which means that he sought to get through to the demons with whom he was accustomed to have dealings. But " God met Balaam "—to his dismay, we doubt not ! He told God of his altars and sacrifices (had not God eyes to see for Himself ?) ; and Jehovah " put a word" in his mouth, and bade him return to Balak and speak it.

A distinguished assemblage awaited Balaam. The King stood by the altars, surrounded by all the princes of his realm. Surely there was never a more momentous occasion in the history of Moab ! Balak had taken much trouble, and gone to considerable expense to get Balaam's assistance. Evidently he had a great opinion of Balaam's influence with the powers of the invisible world. Why did he not call the nation together in its supposed time of peril to y to Baal for help ? Why not convene such a gathering as that on Mount Carmel in Elijah's day, when the prophets of Baal cried for many hours, " O Baal, hear us ? " (1 Kings xviii). Balak judged that the Mesopotamian soothsayer was the most likely person in the world to help him. When Balaam returned from the " bare height " where God intervened and spoke to him, Balak and his princes were full of expectation. What would he say ? Would he pour forth such maledictions as would blast the power of the people they dreaded, so that the armies of Moab and her allies might easily destroy them ? Balaam had used the name of Jehovah quite freely in their hearing, and he had told them that he could only say what He gave him to say ; but all such language was mere jargon to the pagan Moabites. Surely Jehovah could be bought, as all other deities, and was not Balak prepared to pay a high price in order to attain his ends ?

" Balaam took up his parable, and said, Balak, the King of Moab hath brought me from Aram, out of the mountains of the East, saying, Come, curse me Jacob, and come, denounce Israel." Here is a clear statement of what was required. How little did these wicked men realize that they were really calling down a curse upon themselves ! For Jehovah said to Abram when He first called him : " I will bless them that bless thee, and curse him that curseth thee " (Gen. xii. 3). Let all the nations of the earth beware how they see the hurt of the seed of Abraham, however faulty they may be.

Having stated clearly what was expected, Balaam was constrained to say, " How shall I curse whom God hath not cursed ? or how shall I denounce whom Jehovah hath not denounced ? " (J. N. Darby prefers the word " denounce " to " defy "). This should have sufficed to break up the meeting. No success was possible, and the sequel proved that the more the enemies of God's people sought to draw forth a curse against them, the more richly and fully the blessing flowed.

Balaam gave utterance to four parables. Taken together, they give the whole story of God's grace to His people. His wonderful ways are traced from His sovereign choice of them until their ultimate triumph under Christ in the Millennial Kingdom. Each parable has its own theme. In the first is set forth the special and exclusive position in which God had placed His people. " From the top of the rocks I see him, and from the hills I behold him : lo, it is a people that shall dwell alone, and shall not be reckoned among the nations " (Num. xxiii. 9). When God distributed to the nations their inheritance at the time of the Babel-scattering Israel was uppermost in His mind (Deut. xxxii. 7). Israel was to be the centre of His earthly dealings, and the people were meant to be a witness and blessing to all the nations, while divinely separated from them. " Ye shall be holy unto Me : for I Jehovah am holy, and have severed you from the peoples to be Mine " (Lev. xx. 26. J.N.D.). Faith in Solomon responded to this in his prayer at the dedication of the Temple. " They are Thy people, and Thine inheritance, which Thou broughtest forth out of Egypt, from the midst of the furnace of iron . . . Thou didst separate them from among the peoples of the earth, to be Thine inheritance, as Thou spakest by the hand of Moses Thy servant when Thou broughtest our fathers out of Egypt, O Lord God " (1 Kings viii. 51-53). But the people did not value their distinctive place of separation to God, Solomon himself becoming one of the worst transgressors in this respect.

Balaam was speaking " from the top of the rocks," and thus described the people as God in His grace regarded them ; had he walked through the camp and been permitted to record all that he saw and heard there, he would have told a different story, for the ways of the chosen people were scarcely better than those of the heathen Moabites. Israel's distinctive place in the earth has been forfeited by sin ; but it will yet be restored in grace when Christ appears.

Meantime, the Holy Spirit is upon earth forming the Church, the body of the exalted Christ. God is " visiting the Gentiles, to take out of them a people for His name " (Acts xv. 14). The Church belongs to heaven—all its blessings are there ; and it was meant to walk in absolute separation from the world in testimony to Christ. Christians are called " the sanctified " in Heb. ii. 11 ; and the Lord Jesus said of them in John xvii. : " I pray not that Thou shouldest take them out of the world, but that Thou shouldest keep them from the evil. They are not of the world, even as I am not of the world" (John xvii. 15-16). But the Church has been no more faithful in its distinctive place of blessing than Israel in the past. It has been said, and we quote the words with shame : " I looked for the Church and I found it in the world ; I looked for the world, and I found it in the Church."

God wants a separated people. Only through such can He be glorified ; only through the instrumentality of such can He carry out His purposes of love.

Paul told the Galatians that " our Lord Jesus Christ gave Himself for our sins, that He might deliver us from this present evil world according to the will of our God and Father " (Gal. i. 4). He told the Hebrews, " Jesus, that He might sanctify the people with His own blood, suffered without the gate." He followed this with the earnest appeal : " Let us go forth therefore unto Him without the camp, bearing His reproach " (Heb. xiii. 12-13). Shall we not, as individual believers, seek to walk apart from everything that is unsuitable to God and to Christ? Shall we not seek to be sanctified " wholly," that our " whole spirit and soul, and body be preserved blameless unto the coming of our Lord Jesus Christ" ? (1 Thess. v. 23).

The people in their tents knew nothing of what was being said about them in the heights. If God's thoughts of grace had really penetrated their hearts, how different their history would have been !

Balaam concluded his first parable almost enthusiastically (alas, his heart was not in the words that he was constrained to utter !) : " Who can count the dust of Jacob, and the number of the fourth part of Israel ! " Our God is both great and generous ; largeness characterises all His ways of grace. In speaking of the great supper in Luke xiv. 23 He said " that My house may be *filled*." Whether it be earthly or heavenly blessing that is in view, God always contemplates a countless host (Gen. xxii. 17 ; Rev. vii. 9 : xix. 6).

" Let me die the death of the righteous and let my last end be like his : " The life of the righteous had no attraction for him (" he loved the wages of unrighteousness ") ; and had it been in his power he would have consigned millions to perdition ; His end is noted by the Holy Spirit. When the five kings of the Midianites were slain in battle, Balaam perished with them (Num. xxxi. 8). He was a long way from home at that tragic moment ; but death found him amongst the inveterate enemies of the people of God, and still seeking Israel's hurt.

How great the contrast between Balaam, and godly old Simeon in Jerusalem, who, as he held the Babe Jesus in his arms, blessed God, and said : " Lord, now lettest Thou Thy servant depart in peace, according to Thy word ; for mine eyes have seen Thy salvation ! " (Luke ii. 27-30). We shall meet Simeon again, for he appreciated Christ ; but we shall not find Balaam in his company.

(viii) *God's Justified People*

BALAK was astounded and indignant at what Balaam said concerning Israel. " What hast thou done unto me ? I took thee to curse mine enemies, and behold, thou hast blessed them altogether " (Num. xxiii. 11). Balaam could only reply that he was in the hands of Jehovah. Do we marvel that Balak did not immediately expel the prophet from his borders ? Alas, flesh is always foolish and obstinate where God is concerned ! (Rom. i. 22 ; Eph. iv. 18). The King suggested that they should go to another place, and try again. How terribly Satan deceives men made in the image of God whose hearts are not truly subject to Him !

Balak now took Balaam " into the field of Zophim, to the top of Pisgah," and there seven fresh altars were built, and a bullock and a ram was offered on each one. What low and contemptible thoughts both King and prophet had of their Creator, to imagine that such devices and changes of position could revolutionise His mind concerning His people ! The King of Syria and his advisers were just as stupid when they were at war with Israel in the days of Ahab. They suggested that Jehovah was God of the hills, but not of the valleys ; consequently if the Syrians fought on the lower ground, victory would be theirs : (1 Kings xx).

The words " the Lord " should not have been inserted in the Authorised Version of Num. xxiii. 15. Balaam said to Balak, " stand here by thy burnt offering while I meet yonder." He did not go to meet Jehovah ; he did not wish Him to cross his path again. In chap. xxiv. 1 it is expressly said that he went to seek for enchantments " ; but Jehovah, in His love to His people (although unworthy) would not allow this. Accordingly He intervened a second time, and met Balaam. He put a fresh word in his mouth, and said, " Go again unto Balak and speak thus "—It is immense comfort to our souls to note these divine activities. The God with whom we have to do delights to " stand between us and the foe."

Balak's question when Balaam returned to him was remarkable : " What hath Jehovah spoken ? " From what we know of him, he was not willing to submit to whatever it might please Jehovah to say. His hope was that His second message would be more favourable to Moab than the first. What a delightful contrast to this way the attitude of Cornelius and his friends when Peter went to them in Caesarea by their invitation ! " Thou hast well done that thou art come. Now therefore are we all here present before God to hear all things that are commanded thee of God." (Acts x. 33). Such an attitude of soul brings blessing. The whole company listened with avidity to Peter's testimony to the Lord Jesus, and in less than an hour (probably) every person present received the forgiveness of sins, and the gift of the Holy Spirit. In Ezekiel's day some in Israel said to one another : " Come, I pray you, and hear what is the word that cometh forth from Jehovah." They went to Ezekiel and listened to him : they were favoured to hear divine truth, but they were nothing the better for it. Jehovah said to His servant : " Lo, thou art unto them a very lovely song of one that hath a pleasant voice, and can play well on an instrument, for they hear thy words but they do them not " (Ezek. xxxiii. 30-32). A condition distressing in its heartlessness ! May God preserve us from it !

Faith delights to hear what God has to say, and is sure that His word is true. Thus David, when sitting before Jehovah in communion, said : " For Thy word's sake, and according to Thine own heart, hast Thou done all these great things to make Thy servant know them " (2 Sam. 7-21). And when in old age David had to mourn over the unfaithfulness of his own house, he was enabled to say : " Yet He hath made with me an everlasting covenant, ordered in all things and sure ; for this is all my salvation and all my desire, although He make it not to grow " (2 Sam. xxiii. 5). This means that God's revealed counsels were sure whatever His apparent delay in the development of them. All that David looked for awaits the coming in power of the Lord Jesus.

Dear Christian reader, whoever you be in a world of change and upheaval the only sure thing is the word of God. Read it ; meditate upon it ; believe it in its every part. Men are promising one another all sorts of things as we write, and many bewildered souls hope that common sense will yet bring order out of chaos. Nothing but heart-ache lies ahead for those who thus cherish " confidence in flesh." But the counsels of God are sure ; they have Christ for their centre and they will be brought to fruition in God's appointed time.

To return to Balaam. The opening words of his second discourse are exceedingly precious : " Rise up, Balak, and hear ; hearken unto me, thou son of Zippor : God is not a man, that He should lie ; neither the son of man, that He should repent : hath He not said, and shall He not do it ? or hath He spoken, and shall He not make it good ? " (Num. xxiii. 18-19). The wicked speaker is here condemning himself, although probably his seared conscience did not realize it. If God indeed never goes back on His word, why did he consult Him a second time before leaving Mesopotamia ? It is terribly possible to read, and even to utter, words of which we know neither the meaning nor the power ; are we alive to this danger for ourselves ? Are our souls grounded in the great truth of God's unchangeableness ? Psa. cxix. contains 176 verses ; and throughout this long psalm the writer is expressing his confidence in God's word ; and is telling us how sweet it was to his taste, and how much more precious than gold and silver (Balaam would not have agreed with the Psalmist in the last item !)

Balaam's words in Num. xxiii. 19 may well be read again and again. True, the words came from the lips of a bad man, but their source nevertheless was the Spirit of God. There is another Scripture that we must put alongside Num. xxiii. 19. In 1 Sam. xv. 29 when Saul was being rebuked for his disobedience to the command of Jehovah, and was told that the Kingdom would now be rent from him, the prophet added : "the Strength of Israel will not repent, for He is not a man that He should repent." From this solemn passage we learn that God is as faithful and sure in His judgments as in His grace. Solemn consideration for all who are disposed to quibble at His severity (Rom. xi. 22).

Balaam continued : " Behold, I have received commandment to bless ; and He hath blessed, and I cannot reverse it." Here we have an advance on what he said in his first utterance, " God hath not cursed " ; now he passes from the negative to the positive, " He hath blessed " ; but his added words were venomous, " and I cannot reverse it." Gladly would he have done so for reward. But how delightful to our souls to hear the enemy of God's people making public confession that he is powerless to reverse God's grace towards His chosen. " Ye fearful saints, fresh courage take ! "

We come now to the central theme of Jehovah's second message : "He hath not beheld iniquity in Jacob ; neither hath He seen perverseness in Israel." Yet the whole story of the wilderness journey is full of Israel's "iniquity and perverseness." Moses, who loved the people, was obliged to say, " you have been rebellious against Jehovah from the day that I knew you " (Deut. ix. 24). Several of the later prophets traced the perpetual evil of the nation from Egypt to the Captivity. (Read Isa. i. ; Jer. xxxii ; Ezek. xx.). Yet Balaam was instructed to say such wonderful words concerning them from the top of Pisgah ! It is noticeable also that he used the natural name Jacob (" Supplanter ") as well as the name of grace Israel (" prince with God "). God's grace in justifying the ungodly is thus set forth. The full exposition of this wonderful work of God is found in the Epistle to the Romans.

On what principle of righteousness could Jehovah constrain the enemy to say He had not seen iniquity in Jacob, nor perverseness in Israel ? Consider the following precious facts :—(1) On the awful night in Egypt, when God was judging wickedness in the Egyptians He sheltered the Israelites, who were as evil as their oppressors, under the blood of the lamb. Beautiful picture of how God has sheltered us from a more terrible judgment by the blood of Christ. (2) Not long before Balaam came upon the scene, when Jehovah chastised His people for murmuring, He provided for dying sinners the brazen serpent—blessedly typical of the uplifted Son of man by whose death we live, all that we were by nature being judged in His great sacrifice. (3) Moreover, in the midst of Israel's camp stood the Tabernacle, with its blood-stained Mercy-seat. All these things— the lamb, the serpent, and the Mercy-seat—spoke to God of Christ and His perfect work. With Christ before Him, now risen from amongst the dead, and exalted at His own right hand, God is able, consistently with His righteousness, to bless His people, and that abundantly. " He hath made Him sin for us, who knew not sin ; that we might become God's righteousness in Him." (2 Cor. v. 21. J.N.D.).

But is this the whole truth ? Have the faults of God's justified ones no seriousness in His sight ? Will He pass them over lightly, while condemning others severely ? He deals with His own on an exactly opposite principle to this. Sins against grace are more heinous than sins committed in ignorance of grace, and are dealt with by God accordingly. Hence the words in Amos iii. 7 : " You only have I known of all the families of the earth: therefore will I punish you for all your iniquities ? " This is God's government of those in near relationship to Himself. Psalm xc. the first of the fourth (or " Numbers ") book, was written by Moses. He had observed Israel's evil ways in the wilderness, and also Jehovah's governmental chastening of the people, and he says : " Thou hast set our sins before Thee ; our secret sins in the light of Thy countenance " (Psa. xi. 8). Is this a contradiction of Num. xxiii. 19 ? By no means. The enemy was constrained to proclaim *the grace of God* which, resting upon righteous foundations, never varies ; Moses gave expression to *the government of God*. These two truths must be held together in the soul, in order that a proper balance may be maintained. We hope to return to this important matter ere these studies conclude.

Balaam gave utterance to another precious truth concerning the people of God. Not only does He justify them in His grace, but He delights to dwell amongst them. " Jehovah his God is with him." The cloud upon the Tabernacle was proof of this. We have something better than Israel ever imagined. The Holy Spirit is with us. In 1 Cor. vi. 20 we are taught that He dwells in the body of every individual believer, and in 1 Cor. iii. 16 that the saints collectively constitute His temple. " Know ye not that ye are the temple of God, and that the spirit of God dwelleth in you ? " This is the great forgotten truth of the dispensation—one of its greatest marvels, one of its richest blessings, yet practically forgotten ! What power was seen in the Pentecostal Church ! What power would yet be experienced if God's saints could be aroused to the immense fact that His Spirit abides with us still ! In 1 Cor. xiv. 32-25 the case is supposed of a stranger coming into the Assembly of God, and becoming so impressed with the power operating there that the secrets of his heart are laid bare, and falling upon his face he worships God, and reports that God is in His people of a truth !

" The shout of a King is among them," added Balaam. This is anticipative. God already dwelt amongst them in the Tabernacle, but the King is even yet future. Not David is meant, still less Saul, but Christ. He is the King of Jehovah's choice (1 Sam. ii. 10). He will yet reign in Mount Zion, and in Jerusalem, and before His ancients gloriously." (Isa. xxiv. 23).

" God brought them out of Egypt ; He hath as it were the strength of an unicorn (or, buffalo)." How disgraceful therefore their unbelief when they spoke of their enemies as giants, and of themselves as mere grasshoppers in their sight ! " We are not able to go up against the people, for they are stronger than we." Had they measured the Canaanites by the God who brought them out of Egypt they would have spoken differently, but God was not in their thoughts (Num. xiii. 30-33). Caleb and Joshua had no dread of the foe, and both lived to enjoy the blessing of Jehovah in the promised land. Whenever we speak of lack of power, it is to our shame. The Holy Spirit being always with us there is never any lack of power ; but too often there is lack of faith to use the power.

Having said all these wonderful things about the people of God— a people divinely blessed and justified, a people concerning whom God's word is unchanging, a people amongst whom God dwelt in fulness of power—Balaam had to publicly acknowledge that the hellish influences which he had sought to invoke against them were impotent. " Surely there is no enchantment against Jacob, neither is there divination against Israel ; according to this time it shall be

said of Jacob, and of Israel, What hath God wrought ! " (Num.
xxiii. 23). The people of God will be at last triumphant over
every foe, and an abiding monument of divine grace. " Behold
the people shall rise up as a great lion, and lift up himself as a
young lion : he shall not lie down until he eat of the prey, and
drink the blood of the slain."   Micah v. 89 uses similar language
concerning Israel's triumph in the day of Messiah's power. " The
remnant of Jacob shall be among the Gentiles in the midst of many
peoples as a lion amongst the beasts of the forest, as a young lion
amongst the flocks of sheep. Who, if he go through, both treadeth
down, and teareth in pieces, and none can deliver. Thine hand
shall be lifted up upon thine adversaries, and all thine enemies shall
be cut off."

Our ultimate triumph is stated in Rom. xvi. 20 : " the God of
peace shall bruise Satan under your feet shortly." When the last
Adam puts down the persistent disturber of the peace the Church
will be in manifest association with Him.

Of Jacob and of Israel it will yet be said, " What hath God
wrought ! " and concerning the Church it is written, " in the ages
to come He will show the exceeding riches of His grace in His
kindness toward us in Christ Jesus " (Eph. ii. 7).

(ix) *The Beauty and Order of God's People*

WERE it not that we have learned somewhat of the wil-
fulness of the flesh we should be amazed that Balak and
Balaam should make yet another attempt to bring
disaster upon Israel. Balak was very angry at what he had been
obliged to listen to ; but, although he said to Balaam, " Neither
curse them at all, nor bless them at all," he added almost immediately, " Come, I pray thee, I will bring thee to another place :
peradventure it will please God that thou mayest curse me them
from thence." This was obviously sheer wickedness. Jehovah
had already thwarted his plans twice, yet he was determined to make
another effort, Balaam not objecting. Surely the adversaries of
God's people were never more persistent in their hatred than at the
time we are considering !

The new point of view was " the top of Peor, that looks towards
Jeshimon " (meaning, " the waste "). Balaam was this time
constrained to give a truly delightful description of the people as
God saw them ; but the people were not yet in Canaan in restful

possession of every promised blessing, they were still in the desert-wastes. When we examine the New Testament epistles we find wonderful descriptions of God's saints, not only as they will be in heavenly glory eternally, but as they are to-day while in this evil world ! God sees His saints as " in Christ," and faith says exult-ingly, " as He is, so we are in this world " (1 John iv. 17).

Balaam was now fully convinced that it was useless to turn aside any more to seek enchantments. He had proved by experience that the power of Hell is of no avail against the power of God, and that nothing could alienate His heart from the people of His choice. This should have produced in him a broken and contrite spirit, but, alas, it produced no such effect ! The tragedy (for himself, not for Israel) accordingly proceeded to its terrible end.

In Num. xxiv. 2 we read " the Spirit of God came upon him." This may startle some, who may not have learned the distinction of being born of the Spirit, and subsequently and for ever indwelt by the Spirit, and the Spirit of God coming upon an individual. Since Christ accomplished His great sacrificial work, and ascended up on high, the Holy Spirit is God's gift of love to all believers without distinction. Apostles, prophets, evangelists, pastors and teachers no more have the Holy Spirit dwelling within them than the humblest child of God. But, as distinct from this, we sometimes read in the Old Testament records of the Spirit of God coming upon men for some special service. This is the sovereign act of God, irrespective of conversion. Thus the Spirit of Jehovah came upon Othniel (Jud. iii. 10) ; and upon Azariah the prophet in the days of Asa (2 Chron. xv. 1). These were true saints, but we also read that the Spirit of God came upon the messengers of Saul, and even upon the King himself (1 Sam. xix. 20-24). None of these were saints, for murder was in their hearts at the time. In 2 Chron.xxxv. 21 we find God admonishing the pious (but misguided) King Josiah by the instrumentality of the pagen King of Egypt.

In Num. xxiv. therefore we have the Spirit of God coming upon a particularly malicious servant of Satan, taking him completely under His control, and compelling him to describe in glowing terms the beauty of the people of God as God in His grace beheld it ! Wonderful manifestation of divine superiority over all the power of the enemy when we consider that the speaker longed to say the opposite of all that he did say ! With how much more force the words reach our hearts as coming from the lips of such a man as Balaam then if they had flowed from the lips of Moses who loved the people, and who sought their good in every way !

Balaam opened his third parable in peculiarly solemn terms. He describes his own position in relation to God and to the wonderful things he was given to utter. " Balaam the son of Beor saith, and the man of opened eye saith, he saith, who heareth the words of God, who knoweth the knowledge of the Most High, who seeth the vision of the Almighty, who falleth down, and who hath his eyes open." (Darby's translation). The man was thus conscious that with eyes divinely opened he was beholding things in which his heart had no interest. While describing the blessedness and the ultimate triumph of the people that he hated, he knew himself to be a fallen man. Not " fallen into a trance," as the Authorised Version says, but definitely fallen. This privileged but wilful man has gone down to eternal ruin.

We must pause here, and put a question to our own hearts. Is it not possible for us to " see " in an intellectual way, and even to speak of the precious things of God, without our own hearts being moved by them ? As we read God's Word, and get to understand its teaching, let us exercise our hearts and consciences that the truth may get a firm hold of us, and mould and influence our lives. " The eyes of your *heart* being enlightened," is the true rendering of Eph. i. 18. Children of God though we are, let us not neglect the warning of Balaam's unholy handling of the precious things of God.

" Balaam lifted up his eyes, and he saw Israel abiding in tents according to their tribes " (v. 2), and he said, " How goodly are thy tents, O Jacob, and thy tabernacles, O Israel " (v. 5). If the whole of his third parable be read carefully, it will be seen that Balaam begins with the coverings of the people before he speaks of the people themselves. We do not get the pronoun " he " and " his " until we reach ver. 7. These details should be noted. In Exod. xxvi., in the instructions concerning the Tabernacle and its fittings, the various coverings are described as the tabernacle (v. 6) ; the tent (v. 12) ; and the coverings (v. 14). Verses 1-6 speak of the ten fine twined linen curtains with blue, purple and scarlet wrought in them, as the tabernacle ; in verses 7-13 we have the eleven curtains of goat's hair, and they are called the tent—the " ohel " over the " mishcah " ; and verse 14 speaks of the coverings over all of ram's skins died red, and badger's skins. All these things spoke to God of Christ, whose personal perfections cover His people, and secure every blessing for them. How suggestive therefore are Balaam's words : " How goodly are thy tents, O Jacob, and thy tabernacles, O Israel ! " Alas, that the unhappy man was incapable of appreciating the sweetness of what he uttered !

Balaam's third parable is very full. He is describing the beauty, order and blessedness of the people from Jehovah's point of view. Here is a sketch of it:—

What unity ! " The tribes "—v. 2.
What order! "Abiding . . according to their tribes " —v. 2.
What beauty ! " Valleys " : " Gardens "—v. 4.
What fragrance ! " Aloes "—v. 6.
What dignity ! " Cedars "—v. 6.
What sufficiency ! " Beside the waters "—v. 6.
What overflowing ! "Water out of buckets"—v. 7.
What power ! "Unicorn"—v. 8; "Lion"—v. 9.

What Unity ! The twelve tribes were still one whole. The breach which took place after the death of Solomon has not been healed to this day. The tribes will be re-gathered by the sound of the trumpet at the appearing of the Lord Jesus (Matt. xxiv. 31 ; Isa. xxi. 13) It will then be said , " Behold, how good and how pleasant it is for brethren to dwell together in unity" (Psa. cxxxiii. 1). The unity of God's saints in this period is more intimate than that of Israel's tribes. The Spirit of God came from heaven at Pentecost to form it. There is now on earth a wonderful spiritual organism called the body of Christ. All the members are in living union with the glorified Head in heaven, and all are in union with one another. If the truth of this were realized in faith, every true Christian would abandon the ecclesiastical organisations of Christendom, and would never acknowledge any divisive working of any kind again.

What Order ! Balaam saw Israel abiding in tents "according to their tribes." Our God is a God of order. When the five thousand were fed they were not allowed to drop down upon the grass as they pleased ; the Lord Jesus said "make them sit down by fifties in a company" (Luke ix. 14). Israel's camp in the wilderness was planned by Jehovah Himself. The tribes were arranged around the Tabernacle in four groups of three each, under their respective standards (Num. ii.). Even so in the body of Christ every member has been divinely placed and furnished from the infinite resources of the Head in heaven with all that is needful for the blessing and development of the whole, "God hath set the members everyone of them in the body as it hath pleased him" (1 Cor. xii. 18). "The whole body is fitly joined together and compacted by that which every joint supplieth, according to the effectual working in the measure of every part making increase of the body unto the edifying of itself in love " (Eph. iv. 16). How sorrowful to compare God's gracious order with the human machinery which has impoverished the Church for so long !

What Beauty !—" As the valleys are they spread forth, as gardens by the river's side ! " Lovely imagery ! What more beautiful than a valley ; what more attractive than a garden ? The one is suggestive of loveliness, which God always delights to see in His people ; and the other of culture. In Song of Songs iv. 12, the Bridegroom says, " A garden enclosed is my sister-spouse, a spring shut up, a fountain sealed ; thy plants are an orchard of pome-granates, with pleasant fruits " : the bride in response says, " Let my beloved come into his garden, and eat his pleasant fruits " he accepts the loving call, " I am come into my garden, my sister-spouse ! " Israel was God's cultivated garden in the old dispensation ; the Church is His cultivated garden now. Hence the words of the apostle in 1 Cor. iii. 9, " Ye are God's husbandry." Individual saints are His plants, tenderly cared for in infinite wisdom and love. Of mere religionists the Lord Jesus once said, " Every plant which My heavenly Father hath not planted shall be rooted up." (Matt. xv. 13).

Another image of beauty as far as Israel is concerned is found in Ezek. xvi. Jehovah is there remonstrating with the people for their ingratitude. He likens Israel to an outcast babe which he adopted and nourished with gracious care. " Thy renown went forth amongst the nations for thy beauty, for it was perfect through My comeliness which I had put upon thee, saith the Lord Jehovah " (ver. 14). Moses in Psa. xc, says, " Let the beauty of Jehovah our God be upon us." " Thy beautiful flock," said Jehovah reproachfully in Jer. xiii. 20 to the rulers who neglected His people.

We who in this age believe in Jesus stand before God in all the perfection and acceptability of the Risen One. In Col. iii. 12 the apostle uses of Christians the same terms as are used elsewhere of Christ, " The elect of God, holy, and beloved." Compare Isa. xlii. 1, " Behold My servant whom I uphold, mine elect in whom my soul delighteth." In Acts ii. 27 : "Thou wilt not suffer Thine holy One to see corruption." In Matt. iii. 17 : "This is My beloved Son, in whom I am well pleased." Seeing that God in His grace speaks of us as He speaks of His own Son let us " walk as He walked " (1 John ii. 6.). Those who are beautiful before God should also be beautiful before men. Our practical state should correspond to our standing.

What Fragrance!—" As the trees of lign aloes which Jehovah hath planted." Aloes were used for the purposes of fumigation and incense, the wood having a sweet smell. In Psa. xlv, which describes the great King coming forth in His majesty, we read, " All thy garments smell of myrrh and aloes, and cassia." When Joseph of Arimathea and Nicodemus took down the body of our blessed Lord from the cross they wound it in linen cloths, with a hundred pounds weight of myrrh and aloes (John xix. 39-40). Someone has said that the aloe tree is " an image of all that is lovely, fragrant, flourishing, and incorruptible." Wonderful that Jehovah should select this particular tree as setting forth the fragrance of His people in His sight ! On the same principle He bade Moses put pure frankincense upon the twelve loaves which stood continually upon the table of shewbread in the sanctuary (Lev. xxiv. 7). The frankincense upon the meal-offering typified the fragrance of Christ to God (Lev. ii. 2) ; the frankincense upon the twelve loaves teaches us that God's people, viewed as " in Christ," are fragrant as He. This thought should have a profound effect upon our lives. In measure as we are occupied with God and with Christ our lives will be fragrant to those who have to do with us. They will be conscious as they behold our words and ways that we are accustomed to intimacy with God. The very face of Moses when he came down from Mount Sinai revealed the fact that he had been occupied with God (Exod. xxxiv. 29).

What Dignity!—" As cedar trees beside the waters." In the description of the bridegroom (Christ) in Song v. 15 we read, " His countenance (or, bearing) is as Lebanon, excellent as the cedars." In Balaam's third parable the same image of stateliness and dignity is applied to Israel. There has never been on earth so dignified a nation. They stood in special relationship to God, separated from all others ; they possessed His word ; and they were constituted the pivot of His ways in government and blessing (Psa. cxlvii. 19-20). Alas, the people's hearts have never yet entered into the reality of it !

In this era, while Israel is estranged from God, Christians are God's cedars. Every believer in Jesus is a very dignified person indeed—in the divine estimation ! He is a child, son, and heir of God. He stands in nearer relation to God than the most exalted of angelic beings, for he is a member of the royal family of the universe. He will be displayed in majesty with the First-born Son when He comes forth as King of Kings and Lord of Lords to reign.

The world will be amazed at the magnificent display of glory on that day. All this is true of every Christian without distinction ; but the world has no understanding of these marvels. " The world knoweth us not because it knew Him not " (1 John iii. 1). The sense of God's wonderful grace gives moral dignity in our bearing towards men. Carnal pride and pretension is hateful to God, but the moral dignity which results from appreciation of His grace is acceptable in His sight.

What Sufficiency !—" Planted . . . beside the waters." God plants judiciously ; man, not always. God knows that His plants need nourishment, and He places them where they can get it, and moreover provides them with means whereby they can absorb it. There is a suggestion of trees in Col. ii. 7 : " Rooted and built up in Him, and stablished in the faith, as ye have been taught." The rooting is the act of God, and once for all He roots His saints in Christ. Then, like trees, we are built up and established as we draw to ourselves the nourishment divinely provided. This is our responsibility, and it is continuous. There is no lack on God's part. " The river of God is full of water," and it greatly enriches all who draw from it (Psa. lxv. 10). In Christ dwells all the fulness of the Godhead bodily, and we are complete (filled full) in Him (Col. ii. 9-10). One great object for which the epistle to the Colossians was written was to stress the truth that the Christian need not, and should not, go outside of Christ for anything. There was some danger in this respect in Colosse. Other things were being presented to them to be added to their Christianity. " Christ is *all*," says the apostle in ch. iii. 11.

The people of Israel, although planted beside the waters—that is to say, they were in direct relationship with Jehovah, were frequently turning aside from Him, to their own hurt, as well as to His dishonour. But there is a day coming when the people will turn back to the One they have so grievously neglected. They will see God in Christ, and then it will be said : " Jehovah shall guide thee continually, and satisfy thy soul in drought ; and make fat thy bones ; and thou shalt be like a watered garden, like a spring of water, whose waters fail not " (Isa. lviii. 11). In Jer. xxxi. 12 it is added : " They shall come and sing in the height of Zion, and shall flow together to the goodness of Jehovah, for wheat, and for wine, and for oil, and for the young of the flock, and of the herd ; and their soul shall be as a watered garden ; and they shall not sorrow any more at all." Let us avoid Israel's failure, and " hold fast the Head, from whom all the body by joints and bands having nourishment ministered, and knit together, increaseth with the increase of God " (Col. ii. 19).

What Overflowing !—Those who are drawing from the infinite resources of God have something to impart to others. They take in more than they can well contain, hence Balaam's words (although the poor man did not know what he was saying), " he shall pour water out of his buckets, and his seed shall be in many waters." If Balak had understood what he was now hearing he would have had no dread of Israel. The people were intended to be a blessing to all the nations ; they were to spread abroad the knowledge of the one true God ; and to share with others His wonderful grace. Israel has never yet risen to this. How cruelly the Jewish people persecuted Paul because he carried the Gospel to the Gentiles ! " Away with such a fellow from the earth ; it is not fit that he should live " (Acts xxii. 22). In the Kingdom-age their whole attitude will be changed. The beautiful Psalm lxvii expresses the joy of the people as they share their blessings with the nations around them. Micah v. 7 says " the remnant of Jacob shall be in the midst of many peoples as a dew from Jehovah, as the showers upon the grass, that tarrieth not for man, nor waiteth for the sons of men."

While Israel is dry and barren, unblessed by God, and a curse to the world rather than a blessing (Jer. xxvi. 6), believers in Jesus have a fountain of water within themselves springing up into eternal life (John iv. 14) and from them rivers of living water are flowing forth (John vii. 38). This is the power of the Holy Spirit making the things of Christ very real to the Christian, and enabling him to communicate them to others out of the fulness of his heart. The word " buckets " suggests energy in drawing. Where are we as to this ? Are we filling our buckets with the good things of God, and pouring them forth to those around us ? Also, are we making such advance in the spiritual life that we need larger buckets than once we did ? Are we drawing up larger supplies than ever, and pouring them forth abundantly ? " Young men " and " fathers " should be able to handle larger buckets than " babes " (1 John ii. 12-27). " His seed shall be in many waters " expresses the universality of service and testimony for God. " The waters . . . are peoples, and multitudes, and nations, and tongues " (Rev. xvii. 15).

What Power !—The victorious power of the people of God, when Christ takes His place at their head, is the theme of Balaam's final parable ; but he concluded his third utterance with some reference to it : The King and His Kingdom rise up before the prophet's vision. " His King shall be higher than Agag, and His Kingdom shall be exalted." The King here is Christ, higher than earth's highest. Balaam vividly describes the power of God as it acts for, and in His chosen people. " God brought him forth out of Egypt ; he hath as it were the strength of an unicorn (or buffalo); he shall eat up the nations his enemies, and shall break their bones, and pierce them through with his arrows " (ver. 8). For the second time reference is made to the great deliverance from Egypt. The God who broke the power of the enemy at that time will break the power of even mightier foes in the coming day (Micah v. 8).

In Num. xxiv. 9 Balaam was constrained to re-affirm two ancient prophecies concerning Israel. Jacob said of Judah in Gen. xlix. 9 : " Judah is a lion's whelp ; from the prey, my son, thou art gone up ; he stooped down, he couched as a lion, and as an old lion ; who shall rouse him up ? " Balaam said : " He couched, he lay down as a lion, and as a great lion ; who shall stir him up ? " Jehovah said to Abram in Gen. xii. 3 : " I will bless them that bless thee, and curse him that curseth thee." Balaam said : " Blessed is he that blesseth thee, and cursed is he that curseth thee." Thus did the God of Israel confirm His word by the lips of an implacable foe !

If God's earthly people were unconquerable, and superior to all the malice of the enemy, this is yet more blessedly true of God's heavenly saints. We are even now established before Him in Christ the victorious One, and the Holy Spirit dwells within us both individually and collectively. Thus the blessing is full and secure, and the power abundant, may our faith rise up to it all !

(x)   *The Restraining Hand*

THAT Balak should have waited to hear anything more from the lips of Balaam is perhaps surprising, but the hand of God was in it for reasons of His own. Balak was greatly disappointed with the first and second parables ; but after he heard the third, wherein the people he hated described as not only sanctified and justified, but also positively lovely in the eyes of Jehovah, he was furious. " Balak's anger was kindled against Balaam, and he smote his hands together ; and Balak said unto Balaam, I called thee to curse mine enemies ; and, behold, thou hast altogether blessed them these three times " (Num. xxiv. 10).

He now wished to get rid of his visitor. He might indeed have slain him in his fury, but a different end was divinely designed for Balaam ; and, moreover, the full message of God had not yet been delivered. Balak bade him flee to his own country, adding, " I thought to promote thee to great honour ; but, lo, Jehovah hath kept thee back from honour." To all this Balaam's poor covetous heart would regretfully say " Amen." We recall his words to the messengers who waited upon him in Mesopotamia, " Get you into your own land, for Jehovah refuseth to give me leave to go with you " (Num. xxii. 13). Thus, if Balak was disappointed with the result of this extraordinary business, Balaam also was disappointed quite as keenly. But the King having fetched up the soothsayer was not allowed to dismiss him at his will. He had already heard much that was distasteful to him, but he must hear yet more. His own Kingdom of Moab had not been mentioned thus far ; its turn was now coming.

The King, as we would judge, might easily have walked away after giving Balaam his word of dismissal, but Jehovah held him to the spot. There is no other explanation of his remaining there another minute. Also, how else can we explain his silence when Balaam spoke definitely of disaster to his own nation ? The enemy of the people of God had raised a very serious question concerning them, and Jehovah would render his answer in full, and Balak must be made to hear it.

The four parables taken together give the whole story of Jehovah's grace to Israel from the deliverance from Egyptian bondage right onward to Millennial glory and supremacy. It is delightful to our souls to trace it, for Israel's God is also our God ; and He who was so faithful to them in spite of all their disobedience, may be trusted to be faithful to us also. His ways with Israel are leading up to the land of promise for an everlasting possession with Christ as King in their midst; His ways with us are leading up to the Father's house on high.

Balaam reminded Balak that he told him at the beginning that if he would give him his house full of silver and gold he could only say what Jehovah gave him to speak ; and he added, " Now, behold, I go unto my people ; come, I will advertise thee what this people shall do to thy people in the latter days." Balak had no wish to hear more, and Balaam had no wish to say more ; but the power of Hell having been invoked against His chosen people Jehovah had taken the matter up (unasked), and He would see it through to the finish. Moreover, it must finish in His time, and in His way.

Restrained by the power of God, Balak was compelled to listen to a remarkable prediction of earth's final military catastrophe. "The latter days" now come before us.

(xi) *The "Latter Days"*
CHRIST IN POWER: HIS PEOPLE EXALTED

BALAAM'S voice has long since died away.   There is an interval of thirty-five centuries between his days and ours, yet in his final utterance in Moab he spoke of things which are still to come. Who knows the future but God ? With us there is a yesterday, to-day, and to-morrow, but with God the most distant future is as vivid and well-known as the present. He is the great *I am* (Exod. iii. 14), " who calleth the things which be not as though they were " (Rom. iv. 17). In His controversy with Israel concerning the idols of which they were so foolishly enamoured, Jehovah in Isa. xlii. 48 challenges the deities of the heathen to declare " things to come." Thus they would prove themselves to be gods indeed. " I am God, and there is none like *Me*, declaring the end from the beginning, and from ancient times the things that are not yet done, saying, My counsels shall stand ; and I will do all My pleasure " (Isa. xlvi. 9-10).

The politicians of earth grope in the dark. They can only see things as they are at the moment ; their ultimate issues are hidden from them. But children of God who will take the trouble to study the Scriptures, know whither things are tending, and what will be the outcome of them. The greater part of the Bible is occupied with the great crisis which is now approaching, when God will bring forth into manifestation the Man of His choice, and put all things under His sway. Men who know not God, and to whom the Bible is a sealed book, have no resource in their anxieties but alliances and treaties. God's saints, instructed by the Holy Spirit, have no confidence in these devices, and they wait for Christ. This is the proper moral effect of the reverent study of prophecy. " Horns " and " beasts " may be very interesting, and may furnish much material for discussion ; the aim of the Spirit of God in disclosing to us the future is to separate us from man's hopelessly evil order of things, and fix our minds upon Christ.

Balaam opened his last parable by recounting his own privileges— more fully than before. It is painful to read his words, and to realize that one so divinely favoured has perished eternally. " Balaam the son of Beor saith, and the man of opened eyes saith ; he saith who heareth the words of God, who knoweth the knowledge of the Almighty ; who falleth down, and hath his eyes open " (Num. xxiv. 15-16. Darby's Translation. Revised version similar). Some may be disposed to say, " Surely such a man was born of the Spirit, although perverse in his ways, as we ourselves are all too frequently ! " But the New Testament shows us persons may be partakers of even greater privileges than Balaam, and yet fall into such a condition that it is impossible to renew them to repentance. Heb. vi. 4-5 speaks of such persons :—

1. Enlightened.
2. " Have tasted of the heavenly gift."
3. " Made partakers of the Holy Spirit."
4. " Have tasted the good word of God."
5. " And the powers of the world to come."

All these things can be known apart from divine life, and faith in Christ. If the clause " partakers of the Holy Spirit " presents a particular difficulty to some, the reference is to the great truth that the Assembly is the Holy Spirit's dwelling-place (1 Cor. iii. 16). All who take part in such a company, whether real or unreal, are in the presence of that divine Person.

Let none of us be contented with mere externals however good they may be. The essential thing is heart-faith in the Son of God. Ever so little true faith in Him is worth infinitely more than stores of Bible knowledge and Assembly privileges. Balaam's case was the more serious because of the light which shone across his path, but which never penetrated his soul.

It is not unusual for prophets when describing the future to speak in the present tense, as if the great things were even then passing before them. Thus David in Psa. xlv. speaks of the great King as if He were even at that moment riding in majesty, and in Isa. liii. the prophet speaks of the suffering Messiah as if He were then on earth, and experiencing ill at the hands of men. So Balaam in his fourth parable. " I see Him, but not now ; I behold Him, but not nigh " (R.V.). In prophetic vision he saw Christ ; but the Lord Jesus could not say of him what He said to the Jews concerning Abraham : " Your father Abraham rejoiced to see My day ; and he saw it, and was glad " (John viii. 56). It gave Balaam no joy to see Christ, and to be constrained to describe the great day when He will exalt the people Balak hated, and destroy all their enemies, Moab included. Indeed he said, " Alas, who shall live when God doeth this ? " (Num. xxiv. 23). This sounds like a wail of disappointment and despair.

Let us look again at Balaam's words : " I see Him, but not now ; I behold Him, but not nigh." He thus beheld in vision a glorious Person to whom he could never come near. Distance must be his portion for ever, solemn thought ! Nearness to Christ is a very precious privilege. When He comes forth to reign, " at His right hand will stand the Queen in gold of Ophir." (Psa. xliv. 9). This is Israel—" a people near unto Him " (Psa. cxlviii. 14) " It shall be at that day, saith Jehovah, that thou shalt call Me Ishi (my husband), and shalt call Me no more Baali (my master)" (Hosea ii. 16).

The Church will be in a place of greater nearness still. She will be eternally the body and bride of Christ, and the sharer of His heavenly glory, which is immeasurably more wonderful than anything Israel will experience in the land of promise.

In speaking of the coming Christ, Balaam said, " There shall come a Star out of Jacob, and a Sceptre shall arise out of Israel." Here we have the two aspects of His coming. The star is for watchers, and the Church has been called to know Him during " the long dark night." while Israel persists in obdurate unbelief. In Rev. xxii. 16 Jesus says: "I am the Root and Offspring of David, and the bright Morning Star," and to the overcomer in Thyatira He not only promises authority over the nations, but adds, " I will give him the Morning Star " (Rev. ii. 28). Peter distinguishes between the prophetic word, and the Morning Star thus : "We have the prophetic word made surer (by what Peter and his companions saw on the holy mount), to which ye do well taking heed (as to a lamp shining in an obscure place) until the day dawn, and the Morning Star arise in your hearts " (2 Pet. i. 19). The Church will see the coming One at the dawning of the day before the sun shines forth in glorious majesty (Mal. iv. 2). We should ever be on the alert for this ; in spirit like the wise men of Matt. ii. 2 who said, " Where is He that is born King of the Jews ? For we have seen His star in the East, and are come to worship Him." While others slept, these watchers were scanning the heavens for some sign of the approach of the promised One. God graciously responded to their faith, and gave them a star to guide them on their way. Let us not forget the words of the Apostle in 1 Thes. v. 5-6 : " Ye are all the sons of light, and the sons of the day ; we are not of the night nor of darkness. Let us not sleep, as do others, but let us watch, and be sober." We are living far down the dispensation. Man's day, so full of pitiful blunders and desperate sorrows, is drawing to a close. " Knowing the time, that now it is high time to awake out of sleep ; for now is our salvation nearer than when we believed. The night is far spent, the day is at hand : let us therefore cast off the works of darkness, and let us put on the armour of light." (Rom. xiii. 11-12).

Here we must note the various divine titles that were put into the mouth of Balaam. In his first and second parables he spoke of God (" El ") and Jehovah. God ("El ") is suggestive of creative power and Jehovah of covenant relationship.

In his third parable Balaam introduced the name Almighty (" Shaddai ") ; and in his final parable speaks of the Most High (" Elyon ") and the Almighty. The title " Most High " is used frequently in Scripture in connection with the Millennial Kingdom. It teaches us that God is greater than all the petty dignities of earth. He will put them all down in His day, and will dispose of the world as it pleases Him. Who has a greater right to distribute its territories and fix the boundaries of the nations than He who created all things? But how feebly is this understood by earth's statesmen !

Melchizedek, who was a remarkable type of Christ the coming King, spoke of God as " the most High God, Possessor of heaven and earth " (Gen. xiv. 18-19). In Deu. xxxii, where Moses is telling the people of Israel how God distributed territories at the time of the Babel scattering, he also used the title " Most High." In Psa. lxxxiii. 17-18, where Asaph the prophet describes the destruction of Israel's enemies at the end, he says, " Let them be confounded and troubled for ever ; yea, let them be put to shame and perish : that men may know that Thou, whose name is Jehovah, art the *Most High* over all the earth." These thoughts are important, and should be carefully weighed. The earth is full of confusion and sorrow because men in their pride and self-will are bent upon dividing the earth according to their own devices, and to gratify their own ambition. In the intervals of strife, when plenipotentiaries come together to discuss terms of peace, God is not uppermost in their thoughts, still less the Man who is the divinely appointed Heir of all things. New arrangements are made, with possibly some compromises here and there ; but fresh disasters come along all too soon, for the rights of God are not recognised. The nations will yet have to learn that God is the Most High, with absolute right to dispose of everything according to His will ; and as the Almighty He is well able to carry out His will, and crush all opposition.

Balaam was led to describe the conquests of God's King when He appears, and he mentioned Moab first. " He shall smite the corners of Moab." In Dan. xi. 41 where the depredations of the latter-day King of the North are foretold (not to be confounded with Gog— Ezek. xxxviii), we read, " he shall enter into the glorious land, and many countries shall be overthrown : but these shall escape out of his hand, Edom, and Moab, and the chief of the children of Ammon." Why are these ancient enemies of Israel specially named as to escape the heavy hand of the terrible invader ? Because Jehovah had already decreed their destruction by the hands of His own people. Isaiah wrote more than a century before Daniel's day : " they shall lay their hand upon Edom and Moab, and the children of Ammon shall obey them " (Isa. xi. 14). Thus Balak was given to understand that it is not Israel that is doomed to destruction, but his own envious and guilty Moab. But not Moab and her confederates only. He " shall destroy all the children of Sheth (or tumult)." With these words we may connect Psa. lxviii. 30 : " scatter Thou the people that delight in war." The God of peace will not for ever tolerate the doings of " the sons of tumult." Devastated lands, ruined cities, blasted homes, and broken hearts present a sorry spectacle to Him. Self-seeking leaders who are responsible for these conditions, who seek their own aggrandisement at painful cost to others, are utterly abhorent to the God of peace. When the seventh trumpet is sounded (Rev. xi. 15-18) a great shout of triumph will be heard in heaven because the world-kingdom of our Lord and His Christ has at last come. Amongst the many results of the coming of the King it is written : " Thou shalt destroy them that destroy the earth." But ruthless disturbers of the peace will not disappear until that day. One troubler may be cast down, but another will arise, (if not in his place geographically) elsewhere. This has been the world's sad experience ever since the days of Nimrod and Chedorlaomer, the first recorded tyrants.

Israel (i.e. the spared remnant) is destined to play an important part in the subjugation of the enemies of God and His people. Balaam said : " Edom shall be a possession, and Seir also shall be a possession, and Israel shall do valiantly." (Num. xxiii. 18). The destruction of the Western hosts as described in Rev. xix. 19-21, and the overthrow of the hordes of Russia and her Allies as in Ezek. xxxix. will be quite apart from human instrumentality ; but against other foes it is the divine intention to make use of delivered Israel. This is made perfectly clear in Zech. ix. 13 : xii. 6, and other Scriptures, including Isa. xi. 14 already quoted. The long down-trodden sons of Jacob will then become as a lion amongst the nations treading down, and tearing in pieces, with none to deliver (Micah v. 8) " out of Jacob shall come He that shall have dominion, and shall destroy him that remaineth of the city." Led on by Christ, who will then indeed be " a man of war " (Exod. xv. 3 : Psa. xlv. 3-5) Israel's armies will be irresistible. When this work of judgment is completed, Israel will be able to say : " So let all Thine enemies perish, O Jehovah, but let them that love Him be as the sun when he goeth forth in his might " (Judges v. 31).

Balaam's words in Num. xxiv. 19 would seem to be final. What could be added to the statement that " out of Jacob shall come He that shall have dominion," and destroy even the remnants of His peoples' enemies ? But the Spirit of God had still more to say in three short appendices. When Balaam looked on Amalek, " he took up his parable and said, Amalek was the first of the nations, but his latter end shall be that he perish for ever." Ancient prestige, however wonderful it may be in the eyes of men, will count for nothing when God arises in His might.

Next, Balaam " looked on the Kenites, and took up his parable, and said, Strong is thy dwelling-place, and thou puttest thy nest in a rock. Nevertheless the Kenite shall be wasted, until Asshur shall carry thee away captive " (Num. xxiv. 21-22). Great fortifications, strong natural frontiers, and every possible accumulation of military force will be worthless when the day of the Lord opens, for He is wiser and stronger than men. Everything will collapse before Him.

Such triumphs for God and His people found no response in the heart of poor Balaam. Thus he opened his third appendix with the moan, "Alas, who shall live when God doeth this ! " He rightly felt that His intervention will sweep the earth clear of all that which fills men with pride and vain glory. Then in few words he spoke of " Armageddon," where the last terrible clash of the nations is destined to take place. (Rev. xvi. 13-16). That will indeed be the " war to end war ! " " Ships shall come from the land of Chittim, and shall afflict Asshur, and shall afflict Eber, and he also shall perish for ever." " Chittim," strictly speaking, means the island of Cyprus, now in possession of Great Britain ; but in Scripture it is used as a general term for the West (Jer. ii. 10), viewed from the Holy land as God's centre. In Dan. xi. 30 Chittim indisputably means the Roman Empire. Asshur stands for the cruel Assyrian of Isaiah and Micah, the King of the North of Dan. xi. 40. He is at first victorious in the world's last crisis. " Many countries shall

be overthrown " by him (Dan. xi. 41), Jehovah using him as one of
His " carpenters " (Zech. i. 20-21). But both the Assyrian and the
Roman are divinely appointed to destruction. The " he " of
Num. xxiv. 24 is the last head of the Roman Empire (comp : Dan.
vii. 8), the core of which will be the nations of Western Europe—
Britain, France, Italy, Spain, etc. In this blasphemous tyrant, with
his confederate, the false prophet of Rev. xix. 20 (the Antichrist)
all evil will reach its consummation, and both will be despatched
from the battlefield to the lake of fire. In the light of the terrible
doings of recent years (1939-1945) the thought is deeply solemn
that earth's most terrible monsters will not arise out of Germany,
but from amongst the Allied Powers (Russia not included here)
who have toiled and suffered to put Germany down ! How different
would the whole history of earth have been had rulers and people
moved and acted in humble dependence upon God !

(xii) *The "Doctrine of Balaam"*

IN three New Testament epistles Balaam is brought before us as
a warning. Peter speaks of " the *way* of Balaam " (2 Pet.
ii. 15). He is writing severely of false teachers—their evil
doctrines, and their pernicious ways. The Apostle, with eyes
anointed by the Holy Spirit, could see men of the Balaam type
rising up amongst Christians after his departure. The whole chapter
(2 Pet. ii.) should be carefully studied. That holy men such as the
Apostles should have such " successors " is an appalling thought !
Bad teaching can only produce bad living. " The way of Balaam "
was the way of self-will. There was a certain course that he desired
to pursue, which would yield him substantial gain if he were successful ; but his soul knew nothing of humble subjection to the will of
God. Let us beware ! Above all things we must be careful concerning the doctrines that we hold and teach ; but the truth of God
must be allowed to humble us, and subdue every atom of self-will.
Even a dumb ass rebuked the madness of Balaam. God forbid
that we should lay ourselves open to such rebukes !

The Apostle Jude in his short epistle pronounces a threefold
" woe " on the misleaders of the people. " Woe unto them !
for they have gone in the way of Cain, and ran greedily after the
error of Balaam for reward, and perished in the gainsaying of
Korah " (ver. 11). Note the progression in these statements—
" gone " ; " ran greedily after " ; and " perished." The outstand-

ing evils of Christendom are before us in this solemn passage. " *The way of Cain* " was (typically) the rejection of Christ and His death as the only ground of approach to God. Multitudes of persons in the religious world of our own time are following his ruinous example. " *The error of Balaam* " was the corruption of ministry for the sake of personal gain. Balaam has had no lack of successors throughout the centuries. Hirelings in abundance have asserted themselves, caring nothing for the glory of God, nor for the blessing of men. Their own advantage has been uppermost in their thoughts. " *The gainsaying of Korah* " is placed out of its historical order by the Apostle Jude, for he preceded Balaam in the history of Israel (Num. xvi.). But Korah's great sin is mentioned last in the passage before us because of its exceeding seriousness. Men who at the best are only ministers of God challenge the rights of Christ by pretensions to priesthood. The Lord Himself is thus affronted, and the foolish souls who submit to Korahites are kept in spiritual blindness and ignorance, and are cheated of the grace of God to their present and eternal damage. The people, alas, love to have it so. Gorgeously apparalled officials, professedly doing everything for them, appeal to their superstitious folly. The more the study of the Word of God is neglected, the more readily men and women fall into priestly snares.

Many have noted points of similarity between 2 Peter ii. and the epistle of Jude, and some have suggested that one writer copied from the other. This is not correct. Each writer had his own line given to him by the Spirit of God, as everywhere else in Scripture. Peter deals particularly with the *wickedness* of religious leaders (abundantly proved in the pages of " Church " History) ; Jude has in mind their *apostasy*.

The doctrine of Balaam is mentioned by the Lord Himself in His address to the Assembly in Pergamas in Rev. ii. 14. Let us note these distinctions :—

" The *way* of Balaam " in 2 Pet. ii. 15.

" The *error* of Balaam " in Jude 11.

" The *doctrine* of Balaam " in Rev. ii. 14.

Pergamos was one of the seven Assemblies in Asia that were selected and addressed by the Lord Jesus in the second and third chapters of the Apocalypse. There were doubtless Assemblies in the cities named at the time the messages were given by the Lord, and each Assembly needed just the message that was sent ; but

these chapters are part of a prophetic book, and they come therefore within the scope of our Lord's words in Rev. i. 3 : " Blessed
is he that readeth, and they that hear the words of this prophecy,
and keep those things which are written therein : for the time is
at hand." Chapters ii. and iii. are as truly prophetic in character
as the nineteen chapters which follow. The omniscient eye of the
Lord discerned the path that the Church would tread from the days
of the Apostles down to His coming. He beheld sunshine and
shadow, faithfulness and treachery, and He laid it all out for the
guidance of those who have ears to hear, and who desire to do His
will.

Thus He " who has the sharp sword with two edges " said to
Pergamos : " I have a few things against thee, because thou hast
there them that hold the doctrine of Balaam, who taught Balak to
cast a stumbling block before the children of Israel, to eat things
sacrificed to idols, and to commit fornication " (Rev. ii. 14). A
fresh phase of the diabolical conspiracy of Balaam and Balak
against Israel is here exposed. These men had zealously striven
to array the forces of earth and Hell against the people of God, and
their efforts had been turned to confusion by Israel's faithful
Jehovah. The episode concludes in Num. xxiv. 25 thus : " Balaam
rose us and went and returned to his own place ; and Balak also
went his way." But before the soothsayer left his disappointed
patron, he apparently made a vile suggestion to him. If Jehovah
could not be turned away from His people, perhaps the people
could be turned away from Jehovah ! Balaam knew enough of
God to be sure that if the people of Israel could be tempted into
sin Jehovah's hand would come down upon them in judgment.
Thus we read in Num. xxv. 1-2 : " Israel abode in Shittim, and the
people began to commit whoredom with the daughters of Moab.
And they called the people unto the sacrifices of their gods ; and
the people did eat, and bowed down to their gods." Balak was
recommended by Balaam to bring out the women and girls of Moab,
and thus cast a snare before the all too frail people of Jehovah !
Moses became aware of this later, for he referred to it when re-
proving the people for sparing all the women after a campaign
against Midian. " Have ye saved all the women alive ? Behold,
these caused the children of Israel, through the counsel of Balaam,
to commit trespass against Jehovah in the matter of Peor, and there
was a plague among the congregation of Jehovah " (Num. xxxi.
15-16). The record in Num. xxv. 1-9 is painfully solemn ; a great
lesson is here which we must not miss. As surely as Balaam sought

to mingle the people of God with the ungodly in a by-gone age, the teachers of the doctrine of Balaam have laboured to mingle Church and world together in our own era and they have been sadly successful. History is continually repeating itself. Satan first endeavours to destroy, then, finding this impossible he seeks to corrupt, for a pure testimony for God in the earth is abhorrent to him.

In the Apocalyptic Assemblies Pergamos follows Smyrna. In Smyrna we have persecution. In the prophetic view, this refers to the second and third centuries of the earthly history of the Church when the Imperial authorities, urged on by Satan, sought to blot out the name of Christ. A change came when the Emperor Constantine made a profession of Christianity in the early years of the fourth century, and then decided to make the proscribed faith the religion of the State. We must think sympathetically of the saints of that period who, with their forefathers for at least two hundred years, had suffered cruelly for the name of Christ. What relief it must have been to them when the ruling power ceased to be hostile, and professed to be friendly ! It was no longer discreditable and dangerous to be a Christian ; instead, it became positively respectable, and the Bishops and clergy were welcomed at the Imperial Court. But the guile of Satan was in all this, little as the mass perceived it. There was doubtless a spiritual minority who realized the serious tendencies of the changed conditions, and who humbly sought grace from above to be true to their Lord. But the masses were blinded.

The Church was alas no longer to be distinct from the world. It was to be its agent and ally ; indeed, one theologian defined the Church as " the nation in its religious aspect ! " No wonder the Lord said to the Assembly in Pergamos : " I know where thou dwellest, where Satan's throne is " (Rev. ii. 13). Satan's throne is in the world of which he has been the acknowledged prince since the true Prince was cast out (John xvi. 11). To be *in* the world is one thing ; to *dwell* in it, i.e. to settle down and be at home in it, is quite another. We are reminded of the stinging words of James iv. 4 : " Adulteresses ! Know ye not that the friendship of the world is enmity with God ? whosoever therefore will be a friend of the world is the enemy of God."

Let us remind ourselves that we belong to a heavenly order of things. The Church is an exotic in this evil world. On the evening before His death the Lord Jesus said to the Father in the hearing of His disciples : " They are not of the world, even as I am not of the

world. I pray not that thou shouldest take them out of the world,
but that Thou shouldest keep them from the evil. They are not
of the world, even as I am not of the world " (John xvii. 14-16).

To the disciples themselves He said : " If ye were of the world,
the world would love his own : but because ye are not of the world,
but I have chosen you out of the world, therefore the world hateth
you " (John xv. 19). In all His teaching the Lord sought to prepare
them, not for the world's friendship and patronage, but for its
hostility. One great object that He had in mind in giving Himself
up to death was that He might have a people altogether for Himself ;
not bye and bye when earth of necessity has slipped away from us,
but here and now. At great cost He purchased the treasure and the
pearl ; both are now His, and His exclusively. (Matt. xiii. 44-46).

What could be plainer than the words of the Apostle in Gal. i. 3 ?
" The Lord Jesus Christ gave Himself for our sins, that He might
deliver us from the present evil world, according to the will of our
God and Father, to whom be glory for ever and ever. Amen."
In conformity with this, he states his own position definitely in
chap. vi. 14 of the same epistle : " God forbid that I should glory,
save in the cross of our Lord Jesus Christ, by whom the world is
crucified unto me, and I unto the world." To the Hebrew Christians
he wrote that Jesus in order " that He might sanctify the people
with His own blood suffered without the gate." (Heb. xiii. 12). He
went " outside " in His exceeding grace and He wants His people
" outside " with Him, confessing in all their words and ways that
" here we have no continuing city, but we seek one to come."

The question may arise in some minds : " What does Scripture
mean by the world ? Does it refer to the frivolities of the flesh,
and to those lusts and abominations which many decent people
would abhor ? " The scripture term means much more than this. It
includes the whole order of things which Cain and his family
established in independence of God as described in Gen. iv. That
order has developed and expanded, with ramifications religious,
social, political, commercial, scientific, and otherwise. " The
world " may have different forms of manifestation in various lands,
but in principle it is the same throughout, men determined to live
and act in independence of God. The whole order of things here
below which men love and pursue to their eternal ruin, is drastically
described by the Holy Spirit in His warning to saints in 1 John ii.
15-17 : " Love not the world, neither the things that are in the
world. If any man love the world, the love of the Father is not in
him. For all that is in the world, the lust of the flesh, the lust of

the eyes, and the pride of life, is not of the Father, but is of the world. And the world passeth away, and the lust thereof : but he that doeth the will of God abideth for ever." Such language leaves no loophole whatever. Evasion is impossible. The world in all its manifestations is offensive to the Father, and it will come under severe divine judgment ere long.

If the question be asked : " Has not the incoming of Christianity modified conditions amongst men ? May we not now speak of a *Christian* world ? " The opposite is the truth. The incoming of Christianity has made the whole position more serious than before. Men are not only as determined as ever to order their affairs without reference to God, but they have added to their sin and folly the rejection of His beloved Son sent in grace. The shadow of the cross is over all men's undertakings, and that terrible crime must yet be avenged. In Gal. i. 4 the writer speaks of this era as " the present evil age " (not " world ") ; and in 2 Cor. iv. 4 he speaks of Satan as " the god of this age " (not " world ") who blinds men's eyes to prevent the Gospel of the glory of Christ shining into them. Satan was never spoken of in this way until he succeeded in banding together men of all classes to cast out of the world God manifested in flesh (Acts iv. 27). Having accomplished this, he has stepped into the place of the rejected One and is the world's god. Those who profess allegiance to the Lord Jesus, and who confess that they owe everything to His precious blood, should stand sternly apart from the world and its ways, and testify to its evil (John vii. 7). What have the world's political parties, military enterprises, co-operative societies, unions, and combines to do with those who even now are in union with the glorified Christ in heaven as His body, who will shortly be presented to Him as His bride, and who are destined to reign with Him over all things above and below ? " The doctrine of Balaam " would drag us down from our high places, and make us grovel in the dust with those whose interests are exclusively in things below. Definite separation becomes us, and the Lord's promise to those who overcome " the doctrine of Balaam " is singularly sweet and comprehensive. " He that hath an ear, let him hear what the Spirit saith unto the churches " (Mark how individual is this appeal !) To him that overcometh will I give of the hidden manna, and will give him a white stone, and in the stone a new name written, which no man knoweth saving he that receiveth it." (Rev. ii. 17).

The manna—God's gift to Israel in the wilderness—typifies Christ in His humiliation. An omer was to be placed in a golden

pot and laid up before Jehovah in the sanctuary (Exod. xvi. 33).
This suggests that only God knows the whole truth concerning the
Man Christ Jesus. A little has been told to us in the four Gospels ;
but John, when laying down his pen said that if all the things that
Jesus did and said were written the world could not contain the
books. (John xxi. 25). The promise to the overcomer in Pergamos
means that He who was perfect in His separation to God will have
much to tell us about His wonderful pathway when He gets us home.
With what delight shall we listen to His voice !

The white stone, with its new name, private and personal to him
who receives it, is the expression of the Lord's approval. Ample
recompense for every one who has sought to follow His steps in
separation to God, and in obedience to His will !

＊　　＊　　＊　　＊　　＊　　＊

The epistles to the Apocalyptic Assemblies reveal to us how very
early destructive doctrines became established amongst the people
of God. "The doctrine of the Nicolaitanes" ; "the doctrine of
Balaam" ; and the vile teaching of the prophetess Jezebel ! Of
both moral wickedness and doctrinal evil it is written, "a little
leaven leaveneth the whole lump" (1 Cor. v. 6 ; Gal. v. 9). Un-
watchfulness leaves the door open for these things (Jude 4.). May
God in His infinite mercy preserve both writer and reader in moral
and doctrinal purity while we wait for the coming of the Lord
Jesus.

(xiii) *The Government of God*

AN "ecclesiastic" once said to an ardent evangelist : " Say
what you like, your doctrine of free grace tends to careless
living." Such words should not be lightly brushed aside.
Is there any truth in them ? Are all those who boast of their eternal
security conspicuous for holy living ? Or is it not true that in some
cases persons speak with the utmost confidence concerning their
salvation while their ways merit stern reprobation ? But is the
remedy for laxity a general return to legality, with its banks of
cloudy doubts and fears ?

It is important that truth should be well balanced in our minds.
One-sided teaching cannot be expected to yield good results.
There are two lines of truth which should be held with equal firmness
amongst us—the grace of God, and the government of God. These
two lines of truth are found in both Old and New Testaments, in

connection with God's earthly people, and also in connection with His heavenly saints. The grace of God towards Israel shines out brightly in all Balaam's parables, and especially in the words, " He hath not beheld iniquity in Jacob, neither hath He seen perverseness in Israel " (Num. xxiii. 21). Nothing could be allowed to affect this. Jehovah's marvellous grace to Israel was founded upon the blood of the Paschal lamb, and also upon the blood of atonement which was always present on the Mercy-seat. All this spoke to God of Christ. But how great the contrast between Num. xxiii. 21 and chap. xxv. 4 : " Jehovah said unto Moses,: Take all the heads of the people, and hang them up before Jehovah against the sun, that the fierce anger of Jehovah may be turned away from Israel ! " In this terrible passage we have not the grace of God, but the government of God—always righteous, always holy. The people were behaving very wickedly. Israel, which was to stand above, and not be reckoned among the nations, had abandoned their position of separation to God, and had quite forgotten their special relationship to Him. They had come down to the level of the heathen Moabites. They were committing fornication with the women of Moab and Midian, and were worshipping their gods. True, they were not behaving worse than the people around them, and their doings were not scandalous in the eyes of Balak and his princes ; but God's people must " not walk as other Gentiles walk " (Eph. iv. 17). This is true in all dispensations. Israel being in direct and special relationship with Jehovah, came under His heavy hand in discipline. We hear Him saying at a much later date in the history of the nation : " Hear this word that Jehovah hath spoken against you, O children of Israel, against the whole family which I brought up from the land of Egypt, saying, You only have I known of all the families of the earth, therefore will I punish you for all your iniquities " (Amos iii. 1-2).

Nothing could be more equitable than this principle. God could not appear to excuse the shortcomings of the people of His favour. Men of the world frequently do this, but God's ways are always righteous. If He were to exercise leniency towards His own people, how could He judge the world ? And we must never forget that the principalities and powers in the heavenlies are observing with deepest interest His ways with the children of men. (Eph. iii. 10 ; 1 Pet. i. 12).

The vile doings which are recorded in Num. xxv. constituted a particularly dark chapter in Israel's wilderness history, and they brought down a particularly severe chastisement. In later Scriptures Baal-Peor is referred to in terms of the utmost gravity. (See

Josh. xxii. 17 ; Psa. cvi. 29 ; Hos. ix. 10 ; 1 Cor. x. 8). Altogether twenty-four thousand Israelites perished there under the hand of God !

The divine principle enunciated in Amos iii. 1-2 is the explanation of Israel's fearful sufferings during many centuries—sufferings unparalleled in the history of the nations. The end is not yet ; the worst is yet to come.

But when Israel emerges humbled and broken from the final tribulation, the people will acknowledge the righteousness of Jehovah's governmental dealings ; no more will they make their boast in the law ; they will appreciate His grace, fully expressed in the long-rejected Christ. Thus they will become fitted to take their true place at the head of the nations, leading them in paths of righteousness and peace.

Israel's transgressions at Baal-Peor, and the judgment of God which came upon the people in consequence, are specially mentioned in 1 Cor. x. as a warning to all who call upon the name of the Lord in this day. The words of the Apostle are deeply solemn as to this. " All these things happened unto them for examples (or types) ; and they are written for our admonition upon whom the ends of the ages are come. Wherefore let him that thinketh he standeth, take heed lest he fall." The spiritual value of the histories of the Old Testament is thus emphasized ; and it is repeated in Rom. xv. 4.

The same two lines of truth—the grace of God, and the government of God—which we have found in the book of Numbers are found also in the first Epistle to the Corinthians. The condition of the Assembly in Corinth was deplorable when Paul wrote his letter. Almost every form of evil was active there : party strife (ch. i.) ; gross immorality (ch. v.) ; litigation in the world's courts (ch. vi.) ; eating and drinking in the temples of idols (ch. x.) ; gluttony at the Lord's Supper (ch. xi.) ; disorder in speaking (ch. xiv.) ; and dangerous doctrines concerning the resurrection (ch. 15). To all this must be added most improper feelings towards the devoted man who had led them to Christ. Yet with all these terrible evils present to his mind, the Apostle addressed them as " the Church of God which is in Corinth, them that are sanctified in Christ Jesus, saints by calling " (1 Cor. i. 2). Here we have the grace of God strongly expressed. In ch. iii. 9 the Apostle adds : " Ye are God's husbandry (cultivated plot) ; ye are God's building " (His temple). These wonderful figures described the Corinthian brethren *collectively*. God had made them all this in His grace. The writer would not lessen the sense of it in their souls. What

God had made true of them in virtue of Christ and His work formed the basis of his subsequent rebukes and appeals.

In ch. vi. the grace of God to the Corinthians *individually* is strikingly set forth. We must remember that the majority of the saints in the Assembly in Corinth were formerly heathen ; Jews were not numerous amongst them. The Greeks of that day were undoubtedly polished and educated. Their works of art are the admiration of men still. But along with all this there was the deepest moral degradation, fruit of the idolatry which had covered the earth for ages. Paul was divinely encouraged to persevere in his work in Corinth, spite of opposition. The Lord said to him, " I have much people in this city " (Acts xviii. 10). Out of the terrible filth at Corinth he picked up pearls which will be the delight of his Lord for ever. But meantime things were not going well there. Paul had not felt led to build himself a house in Corinth, and settle down amongst the believers. He formed them into an Assembly, instructed them as to their new privileges and duties, and left them to their own responsibility, assured that the Holy Spirit would take care of them, if they would look to Him in faith. This they failed to do ; hence the sorrow with which the Apostle addressed his first letter to them. Nevertheless, spite of their failure, he set forth the grace of God very strongly. In chap. vi. 11, after mentioning some of the most abominable evils into which the Corinthian people in general had sunk, he said : " And such were some of you—but ye are washed, but ye are sanctified, but ye are justified, in the name of the Lord Jesus, and by the Spirit of our God." Had the Corinthians been in the enjoyment of all this, they might well have burst forth into praise in some such words as these (happily familiar to many who will read these pages) :—

> O God of matchless grace,
> We sing unto Thy name !
> We stand accepted in the place
> That none but Christ could claim.
> Our willing hearts have heard Thy voice,
> And in Thy mercy we rejoice.

> 'Tis meet that Thy delight
> Should centre in Thy Son !
> That Thou should'st place us in Thy sight
> In Him, Thy Holy One !

Thy perfect love has cast out fear,
Thy favour shines upon us here !

(HANNAH K. BURLINGHAM)

A further precious setting forth of grace is found in 1 Cor. vi. 19 : " What ? Know ye not that your body is the temple of the Holy Spirit, which is in you, which ye have of God, and ye are not your own ? For ye are bought with a price." The words " Know ye not ? " repeated six times in this chapter, were intended as reminders of the great things the Corinthians had been taught, but which they were letting slip. Terrible danger for us also !

As surely as Jehovah in His holiness resented the transgressions of the people of Israel in Balaam's day—" a people near unto Him " (Psa. cxlviii. 14), so did the Holy God resent the transgressions of the Corinthian saints, a people nearer still to Him, and more richly blessed than Israel ever imagined—chastisement followed in both cases.

Paul reminded the Corinthians that the saints will judge the world, and even angels, in the coming day (1 Cor. vi. 2-3). With such a destiny before us, dare we in our ways come down to the world's level ? In warning the Colossians against fleshly corruption, the Apostle said, " for which things sake the wrath of God cometh on the sons of disobedience, in which ye also walked once when ye lived in them " (Col. iii. 7). He wrote similarly to the Ephesians (Eph. v. 6). The *wrath* of God will not come down upon God's saints, however faulty they may be (the blood of Christ secures us from that) ; but the *judgment* of God in the form of chastening is certain if we do not judge ourselves. Some in the Corinthian Assembly were proving the truth of it. " For this cause many are weak and sickly among you, and many sleep " (1 Cor. xi. 30). Their conduct was not necessarily worse than that of others around them. In that licentious seaport multitudes were doubtless guilty of all the evils which are condemned in Paul's Epistle, yet perhaps the hand of God did not come down upon them in the marked way that is described in the verse just quoted. The sins of the ungodly are all noted in God's books, and will be dealt with at the Great White Throne (Rev. xx. 12). God's redeemed will not be there, having been glorified long before ; our judgment is here and now, " that we should not be condemned with the world " (1 Cor. xi. 32).

The government of God is one of the principal themes in the writings of Peter. In his first epistle the children of God are in view, and in his second epistle the world is before him. In exhorting the children of God to be holy, the Apostle says, " If ye call Him Father who without respect of persons judgeth according to every man's work, pass the time of your sojourning here in fear" (1 Pet i. 17). Fathers, young men, and babes ; preachers and teachers and their hearers, all alike live under the eye of the Father, who takes account of all our ways. A careful walk becomes us. The whole " time of our sojourning here " has its dangers ; and the Father's holy hand corrects us as we need it. In Peter's fourth chapter (ver. 17) he says : " The time is come that judgment must begin at the House of God (" whose house are we "—Heb. iii. 6) ; and if it first begin at us, what shall the end be of them that obey not the gospel of God ? " In Ezekiel's day, when Jehovah could no longer forbear, and felt constrained to smite, He said : " Begin at My sanctuary " (Ezek. ix. 6). When Nadab and Abihu were destroyed for offering strange fire before Jehovah, Moses said unto Aaron, " This is that Jehovah spake, saying, I will be sanctified in them that come nigh Me, and before all the people I will be glorified" (Lev. x. 3). It is true in every dispensation that " God is greatly to be feared in the assembly of the saints, and to be had in reverence of all them that are about Him " (Psa. lxxxix. 7). The Corinthian brethren forgot this ; hence the calamities which overtook them in the holy government of God. If we become indifferent to His honour, He will take up matters with us, and thus vindicate His great name.

Peter raises a serious question in this connection : " What shall the end be of them that obey not the gospel of God ? And if the righteous scarcely (i.e. with difficulty) be saved, where shall the ungodly and the sinner appear ? " (1 Pet. iv. 17-18). The question is answered in the writer's second epistle. " The heavens and the earth, which are now, by the same word (the word of God) are kept in store, reserved unto fire against the day of judgment and perdition of ungodly men . . . The day of the Lord will come as a thief in the night, in which the heavens shall pass away with a great noise, and the elements shall melt with fervent heat, the earth also and the works that are therein shall be burned up " (2 Pet. iii. 7-10). Thus no evil will be indefinitely spared. Whatever the long-suffering of God, judgment is certain upon sinners and saint alike. For the one it is irretrievable ruin, for the other it is present chastening in order that we may become partakers of the holiness of the One Who uses the rod (Heb. xii. 10). The path of the believer through an evil world, with a principle of evil within himself ever ready to respond to the evil around, is not easy. Yea, it is difficult, and indeed impossible apart from sustaining grace (Matt. xix. 26). But the humble confiding soul need not fear. Greater is the power (of the Holy Spirit) within him than all the power that can be arrayed against him (1 John iv. 4). Glory is as certain for the believer in Jesus as eternal judgment is sure for all who " obey not the gospel of God."

.   .   .   .

What important principles of truth are laid open to us in the ancient history of Balaam the son of Beor !

(1) The sovereign grace of God, which neither the malice of the enemy nor the unfaithfulness of God's people can ever affect ! This, as regards Israel, was proclaimed by hostile lips, on enemy ground, and in the hearing of the would-be destroyer !

(2) The righteous judgment of God against those whom He brings near to Himself.

(3) The inveterate (but futile) hatred of the powers of darkness against the objects of God's favour.

(4) The watchful interest of God in His own, even when astray from the path of holiness. Unasked, He places Himself between them, and all who would do them harm. " Blessed be God our God."